EVALUATING USABILITY OF HUMAN–COMPUTER INTERFACES:
A Practical Method

EVALUATING USABILITY OF HUMAN–COMPUTER INTERFACES:
A Practical Method

SUSANNAH J. RAVDEN
Ciba-Geigy Plastics, Duxford, Cambridge

GRAHAM I. JOHNSON
MRC/ESRC Social and Applied Psychology Unit
University of Sheffield, Sheffield

ELLIS HORWOOD LIMITED
Publishers · Chichester

Halsted Press: a division of
JOHN WILEY & SONS
New York · Chichester · Brisbane · Toronto

First published in 1989
ELLIS HORWOOD LIMITED
Market Cross House, Cooper Street,
Chichester, West Sussex, PO19 1EB, England
The publisher's colophon is reproduced from James Gillison's drawing of the ancient Market Cross, Chichester.

Distributors:

Australia and New Zealand:
JACARANDA WILEY LIMITED
GPO Box 859, Brisbane, Queensland 4001, Australia

Canada:
JOHN WILEY & SONS CANADA LIMITED
22 Worcester Road, Rexdale, Ontario, Canada

Europe and Africa:
JOHN WILEY & SONS LIMITED
Baffins Lane, Chichester, West Sussex, England

North and South America and the rest of the world:
Halsted Press: a division of
JOHN WILEY & SONS
605 Third Avenue, New York, NY 10158, USA

South-East Asia
JOHN WILEY & SONS (SEA) PTE LIMITED
37 Jalan Pemimpin # 05–04
Block B, Union Industrial Building, Singapore 2057

Indian Subcontinent
WILEY EASTERN LIMITED
4835/24 Ansari Road
Daryaganj, New Delhi 110002, India

© **1989 G. Johnson and S. Ravden/Ellis Horwood Limited**

Library of Congress Card No. 98–2109

A CIP Catalogue Record for this book is available from the British Library

ISBN 0–7458–0614–7 (Ellis Horwood Limited)
ISBN 0–470–21496–1 (Halsted Press)

Typeset in Times by Ellis Horwood Limited
Printed in Great Britian by Unwin Bros., Woking

Table of contents

Preface

This book describes a practical method for the evaluation of human–computer interfaces, with the aim of assessing 'usability' of computer-based application systems, both during and after development.

What do we mean by the 'human–computer interface'?
This refers to the programmable, or software, interface which enables an end-user (i.e. the person using the computer) to access and interact with a computer application system, to make use of the facilities and functions which it provides, and to carry out the tasks for which the system has been designed.

What do we mean by 'usability'?
This concerns the extent to which an end-user is able to carry out required tasks successfully, and without difficulty, using the computer application system.

How does the human–computer interface influence usability?
The human–computer interface, or 'user interface', represents the only part of the application system with which the end-user comes into direct contact. It therefore plays a vital role in enabling the human to 'use' the system.

Who should read this book?
The book is aimed primarily at those people who are directly involved in the design, development and evaluation of human–computer application system interfaces, and in assessing usability. It is also of relevance to those who may be evaluating one or more application systems with a view to purchase.

A secondary readership may include reseachers, teachers and students within disciplines such as information technology, computer science, systems and software engineering, and in areas such as human factors and ergonomics.

Why is the book important to practitioners?
Academic disciplines, such as applied psychology, ergonomics, human factors, cognitive psychology, and so on, are producing a steady stream of literature on human–computer interaction.

However, practitioners still voice frustration and confusion at the scarcity of practical, systematic methods which they can actually use to evaluate human–computer interfaces. There is even less available to assist in evaluating user interfaces and usability during the complex process of design and development. As awareness of the importance of user interface design continues to grow, the need to translate the findings of contemporary academic research into useful methods for practitioners is becoming more urgent.

Although the method described in this book has its roots within these academic disciplines, the way in which it presents its material, and the language it uses, aims to bridge the gap which exists between research and practice. The book therefore presents much of the current guidance emerging from the academic research community in a straightforward manner accessible to practitioners.

HOW THE BOOK IS ORGANIZED
The book is structured in three main parts.

Part I describes the ideas behind the method, including why and how it was developed (Chapter 1), and provides a brief overview of its main features, including the evaluation checklist on which the method is based (Chapter 2).

Part II explains the evaluation checklist in detail. In Chapter 3, the checklist is presented, with accompanying instructions. Chapter 4 provides detailed explanations of each section within the checklist.

Part III explains how to carry out an evaluation using the method. Chapter 5 provides detailed information on how to construct tasks for use in the evaluation; Chapter 6 describes how to conduct the evaluation; and Chapter 7 provides some guidance on how to extract and analyse the results of an evaluation.

The Appendix provides brief illustrations, in the form of case studies, of how the method has been used in different contexts. The book ends with a bibliography, which provides useful sources for further reading.

Acknowledgements

We are indebted to the design engineers with whom we have worked in ESPRIT (European Strategic Programme for Research and Development into Information Technology) over the last three years, whose feedback during development of the method proved invaluable, and whose enthusiasm for it prompted the decision to translate it into book form.

We must also thank our colleagues at the MRC/ESRC Social and Applied Psychology Unit, at Sheffield University. We owe special thanks, in particular, to Chris Clegg, for his immense support and encouragement, and to Debby Lynch, whose tolerance, speed and hard work in helping us prepare the book has been invaluable.

Part I
Introduction and background to the method

Part I describes the background to the method and its development, and provides a brief summary of its main features.

1.   The ideas behind the method
This briefly describes the background to the method, outlining the reasons why it is needed, how it has developed, and the potential benefits of using it.

2.   Overview of the method
This describes the key features of the method, including the evaluation checklist, the need to evaluate usability in the context of tasks, and the benefits to be gained from including end-users and others in the evaluation.

1

The ideas behind the method

1.1 USABILITY AND USER INTERFACE DESIGN

As organizations grow increasingly dependent on computer application systems, the ability of the end-users of these systems to use them effectively becomes critical, in some cases to successful functioning of the whole organization. If end-users find that the system actually interferes with, rather than enhances, their work, and if it causes them undue stress and frustration, then they may find it inefficient to use, and may actually cease to use it altogether.

The programmable, or software, interface which allows interaction between end-users and the computer, plays a vital role in the effectiveness with which a human–computer system functions. The user interface generally consists of information displayed to the user and facilities which allow the user to enter information into the computer, to manipulate information which is displayed, and to take control actions. It enables the end-user to access and make use of the facilities and functions which the system provides, and to carry out the tasks for which it has been designed. It provides the user with information about the system, about what it does, and about what the user can and should do. It enables the user to learn about the system and to build an understanding of how it works.

If this interface is poorly designed, it can severely restrict the user's ability to use the system. It can cause confusion and frustration, difficulty in learning how to use the system, misunderstanding of what the system is doing and of what the user should do, errors, and difficulty in using the system to carry out tasks successfully.

It is therefore essential that the user interface meets the needs of those using the system to carry out tasks. A large, and increasing, body of research, recognizing the need for 'user-centred' design, is currently investigating how the user interface should be designed in order to meet these needs. This area of research is generally known as 'software ergonomics' (or 'cognitive ergonomics'), and falls within the discipline of 'ergonomics' (or 'human factors').

1.2 THE CONTRIBUTION OF ERGONOMICS

Ergonomics is concerned with 'designing for human use' (McCormick and Sanders, 1983, p. vii). It aims to 'maximise safety, efficiency and comfort by matching the requirements of the operator's 'machine' (or indeed any aspects of his workplace which he has to use) to his capabilities' (Oborne, 1982, p. 7). Software ergonomics forms a branch of ergonomics, and is concerned specifically with the human–computer software interface.

The literature in the area of software ergonomics is extensive, and growing rapidly. Many attempts have been made to present the research knowledge emerging from the discipline in a practical form, for use by those designing and developing human–computer interfaces. A frequently used approach is to present it in the form of 'guidelines' for design (e.g. Gardner and Christie, 1987; Smith and Mosier, 1986). Guidelines vary enormously within the literature, both in content and in level of detail. Some are fairly general statements of overall principles, and others are highly detailed. Some of the most comprehensive sets of guidelines for software-interface design, have been produced over the years by the Mitre Corporation, for the US Air Force. Each successive report revises and expands on the previous one, and the most recent contains 944 design guidelines (Smith and Mosier, 1986).

However, although the details of the many guidelines within the literature vary, the underlying principles, or criteria, for 'good' user interface design, on which they are based, are generally in agreement.

1.3 THE NEED FOR A PRACTICAL METHOD FOR ASSESSING USABILITY

The ultimate aim in producing guidance for well-designed user interfaces must be to improve usability of the system for the user. However, guidelines rarely concern the needs and requirements imposed on the interface by the tasks which an end-user carries out in a particular context. In addition, the presentation of guidelines generally includes very little guidance concerning where, when and how to use them, and how to apply them in a particular situation.

Guidelines therefore have a limited use as a means of evaluating the effectiveness of a user interface when carrying out tasks. In order to enable the research findings emerging in this area to be applied in assessing usability, a method is needed which goes beyond lists of design guidelines, but which utilizes relevant material existing within them.

This book aims to provide such a method. This requires those evaluating an interface (i.e. 'evaluators') to carry out realistic tasks using the system, as part of the evaluation. It provides a structured and systematic tool, in the form of a checklist, with which to apply the knowledge emanating from software ergonomics research to evaluation of user interfaces. The method, and in particular the nature of the checklist, enables an interface to be evaluated by a variety of people, with differing expertise and backgrounds, including, for example, interface designers and other technical experts, and, most importantly, representative end-users, who may, or will, actually use the system in practice.

The method does not aim to solve problems, or to enable a quantitative assessment of usability (e.g. by adding up scores). It provides a means of identifying problem areas, of extracting information on problems, difficulties, weaknesses, areas for improvement, and so on.

1.4 DEVELOPMENT OF THE EVALUATION METHOD

The development of the method described in this book took place predominantly during collaborative research and development between ourselves (as part of a group of applied psychology researchers at the MRC/ESRC Social and Applied Psychology Unit, Sheffield University) and other participants within two major projects within ESPRIT (European Strategic Programme for Research and Development into Information Technology). These projects were The Development of an Automated Flexible Assembly Cell and Associated Human Factors Study (Project No. 534, 1984–1988); and Human-Centred CIM Systems (Project No. 1217/1199, 1986–1989).

One of our main roles within these projects was to develop practical 'tools', for use by those designing and developing computer-based application systems, including user interfaces. The method described here forms one of these tools. Throughout its development, it benefited considerably from the invaluable feedback provided by the other project participants, predominantly design engineers, with whom we collaborated.

Through our ESPRIT work, it became apparent that the method which we have developed was providing these technical practitioners with a much-needed, practical and 'usable' tool, which they could actually apply in practice, with success, to evaluate user interfaces and to assess usability. Although the material on which the method is based is not new, they found that the way in which it is presented and used enabled them to understand and to make use of this material.

1.5   POTENTIAL FINANCIAL BENEFITS OF USING THE METHOD

User interface evaluation using the method may incur some immediate financial costs; for example, where the development process is lengthened, or through the involvement of end-users and others in the evaluation.

However, the importance of user interface design and of usability should not be underestimated, and its evaluation should be expected to take the time and effort worthy of this importance. In the longer term, the benefits which are likely to result from the evaluation may outweigh the costs. Benefits may include, for example:

— reduced training time for end-users;
— reduced support costs, due to fewer, and less significant, difficulties,
— reduced need for amendments, modifications and revisions after implementation;
— where relevant, increased sales, as a more usable, well-designed and acceptable product is produced;
— a greater willingness among end-users to accept the system and to use it effectively;
— greater efficiency and utilization of computer resources;
— a greater awareness, amongst those developing computer application systems, of the requirements for 'user-centred' design.

2

Overview of the method

2.1 THE EVALUATION CHECKLIST

The method is based on a practical tool, in the form of a checklist. This is based on a set of software ergonomics criteria, or 'goals', which a well-designed user interface should aim to meet. The checklist consists of sets of specific questions aimed at assessing usability. These provide a standardized and systematic means of enabling those evaluating an interface to identify and 'make explicit' problem areas, areas for improvement, particularly good aspects, and so on.

2.1.1 Composition of the checklist

Part II of the book describes the checklist in detail; Chapter 3 presents the checklist itself, together with detailed instructions on how to complete it; and Chapter 4 provides a detailed explanation of each criterion, and of each checklist question. The following therefore gives only a brief overview of the composition of the checklist.

Each of the first nine sections is based on a criterion, or 'goal', which a well-designed user interface should aim to meet. The criterion is described at the beginning of the section, and a number of checklist questions follow, which aim to identify whether the interface meets the criterion. The criteria are not in any order of importance within the checklist. The nine criteria are as follows:

Section 1 — Visual clarity;
Section 2 — Consistency;

Section 3 — Compatibility;
Section 4 — Informative feedback;
Section 5 — Explicitness;
Section 6 — Appropriate functionality;
Section 7 — Flexibility and control;
Section 8 — Error prevention and correction;
Section 9 — User guidance and support.

When answering a checklist question, the evaluator ticks one of four alternative options. Of these, 'always' is the most favourable reply, and 'never' is the least favourable. The other two options are 'most of the time' and 'some of the time'. There is space beside each question for the evaluator to make any comments of relevance to the question and to their answer.

At the end of each section, space is provided for the evaluator to add any other comments, good or bad, of relevance to the issues raised within the section. This is followed by a five-point rating scale, ranging from 'very satisfactory' to 'very unsatisfactory', which enables the evaluator to give a general assessment of the interface in terms of the criterion and questions within the section.

Section 10 is specifically concerned with usability problems that the evaluator encountered when carrying out the tasks. For each question, the evaluator indicates whether there were major, minor or no problems.

Section 11 consists of general questions on system usability. The questions are 'open', allowing the evaluator to express opinions of various factors, including the best and worst aspects of the system, those aspects which caused most difficulty, any suggested improvements, and so on.

2.1.2 Sources of the checklist questions

The checklists have been developed with reference to a number of sources, and it is important that these are noted here.

A number of questions within Sections 10 and 11 are taken directly from the 'Usability: Screening Questionnaire' in Clegg *et al.* (1988, Chapter 6), and the format for these sections, and for the questions within them, have been adapted from this source. In addition, early versions of Clegg *et al.* (1988) provided the stimulus for a number of questions within Sections 1 and 9.

Other sources for the checklist include, amongst others, Smith and Mosier (1986), Gardner and Christie (1987) and Shneiderman (1987).

2.2   HOW SHOULD THE CHECKLIST BE USED? — THE IMPORTANCE OF EVALUATION TASKS

A key feature of the method, and a prerequisite for using the checklist, is that the evaluator uses the system to carry out tasks which it has been designed to perform, as part of the evaluation. This takes place before completing the checklist, and represents the first step in the evaluation.

Tasks used in the evaluation should be representative of the work which is to be carried out using the system, and should test as much of the system, and as many of its functions, as possible. Such tasks require careful construction (this is detailed in Chapter 5) and are extremely important to the validity of the user interface evaluation. There are a number of reasons for this.

(1) Tasks which are realistic and representative of the work for which the system has been designed provide the most effective way of demonstrating the system's functionality.
(2) This approach enables those evaluating the interface to see it not simply as a series of screens and actions, but as part of the application system as a whole.
(3) By carrying out tasks, evaluators can be exposed to as many aspects of the user interface as possible, which is necessary if they are to comment usefully, and in detail, on specific features, problems, strengths and deficiencies.
(4) Many significant problems and difficulties are only revealed when carrying out tasks.
(5) In some cases, there may be important aspects of usability which can only be captured by using the system (e.g. inflexibility of a menu structure when the task requires rapid movement between different parts of the system).

In addition to the above points, important information can be gathered by observing an evaluator's performance when carrying out tasks in an evaluation. Observation and recording of task performance is extremely valuable in identifying those difficulties which evaluators experience when interacting with the system. As a supplement to the completed checklists, this information can enable, for example, investigation of critical confusions, common mistakes, and so on; examination of differences between evaluator responses to checklist questions, by referring to the task data; examination of task data for supporting evidence of an evaluator's comments about the interface; and comparison of evaluator groups according to their task performance.

2.3   WHO SHOULD BE INVOLVED IN THE EVALUATION?

The method enables a variety of different people, with different backgrounds and expertise, to evaluate the same user interface. A particular benefit of this is that it enables end-users who will use the system in practice to assess its usability before it is implemented.

The need to involve end-users in the design and evaluation of computer-based systems has been stressed frequently within the literature (e.g. Mumford, 1983; Gould and Lewis, 1985). End-users bring job-specific knowledge to an evaluation. They can supply relevant and accurate details of the nature of tasks and difficulties which they regularly encounter, providing valuable insights.

End-users may provide feedback on whether the interface will be adequate in a real working situation. They can identify whether the interface is compatible with user conventions, such as layout, labelling, terminology, units of working, and so on. Actual knowledge of task requirements in a working situation may reveal, for example, parts of the interface where certain information is necessary but is currently not available, or places where simultaneous access to certain information may be required, but is not currently allowed by the interface.

The degree of end-user involvement which is possible will depend, to a large extent, on the context of the evaluation. For example, factors such as the general availability of end-users, the scale and budget for the evaluation and the degree of novelty and complexity of the application may all influence the scope of user involvement.

In addition to representative end-users and to the actual interface designer, other evaluators may be, for example, software engineers not involved in the design and development of the interface being evaluated, who can provide an objective viewpoint from a more technical perspective; or experts in human-related issues, who can provide knowledge and understanding of the potential psychological implications of different designs.

2.4   WHEN CAN THE METHOD BE USED?

The method can be used to evaluate usability both during and after design and development of the user interface.

Where prototyping tools are available, it can enable early evaluation of an interface, or of alternative interfaces, by representative end-users and others, so providing feedback at early stages in the design process. In this way, different configurations can be tested, and necessary improvements made, before reaching a fully operational state ready for implementation. At the later stages of development, it is more difficult to make major modifications to the interface.

Certain aspects of the method can still be of value where prototyping tools are not available, and where the system has not yet been developed sufficiently for tasks to be carried out realistically, and for representative end-users to be involved. The checklist can be of benefit by identifying user-centred goals (the criteria) and sub-goals (the checklist questions) for the interface designer.

The method can be of particular value in the later stages of development, where the sytem is sufficiently developed to enable realistic tasks to be carried out. Similarly, it can be used to evaluate a system after development and before implementation. This may be particularly valuable, for example, where a system has been developed elsewhere, or purchased, and requires amendment, modification, or improvement before implementation.

The method can also be used in evaluating an application package with a view to purchase. Here tasks can help to assess whether the system meets the required functionality, and the evaluation can highlight good and bad features, aspects which are unsatisfactory, those which are particularly excellent, and so on. The method can also be used to evaluate alternatives for purchase, as it can allow a comparison between them.

In certain situations the checklist may not be sufficient to cover all the important usability issues which should be assessed in a particular evaluation. For example, where an interface relies upon speech input/output, some checklist questions will not be entirely appropriate and others may be added. The same may be true for systems which do not employ mainstream, relatively conventional user interfaces.

It may be possible to augment or 'tailor' the checklist in these cases. Great care must be taken if augmenting the checklist, however, in order to preserve its underlying principles. As far as is possible, any additional questions should follow the general criteria outlined at the beginning of Sections 1 to 9 ('Visual clarity', 'Consistency', etc.). Other modifications, such as shortening the checklist, should also be made with extreme care.

Part II
The evaluation checklist in detail

Part II presents the evaluation checklist, and describes it in detail.

3. The evaluation checklist
This presents the full evaluation checklist, with accompanying instructions for its completion.

4. Detailed explanations of criterion-based sections
For each section, the criterion itself is described, followed by a brief explanation of each question within that section.

3

The evaluation checklist

INSTRUCTIONS FOR COMPLETING THE CHECKLIST

Sections 1 to 9: criterion-based questions

(1) Each of these sections is based on a different criterion, or 'goal', which a well-designed user interface should aim to meet. The criterion is described at the beginning of the section, and consists of:
   — a heading (e.g. 'Visual clarity'), followed by
   — a statement (e.g. 'Information displayed on the screen should be clear, well-organized, unambiguous and easy to read').

(2) A number of checklist questions follow, and these aim to assess whether the user interface meets the criterion.

For example, in Section 1 ('Visual clarity'), the questions check whether information which is displayed on the screen is clear, well-organized, unambiguous and easy to read.

(3) To the right of the checklist questions, you will see four columns, labelled **'Always'**, **'Most of the time'**, **'Some of the time'** and **'Never'**.

For each checklist question, please tick the column which best describes your answer to the question.

(4) Then write any comments which you feel you could make when answering a checklist question, in the column labelled: **'Comments'**.

For example, when answering question 12 in Section 1: 'Is information on the screen easy to see and read?', you may tick the column 'some of the time', and you may mention particular screens where information was very difficult to see and read, in the 'Comments' column.

(5) If you feel that a checklist question is not relevant to the interface which you are evaluating (e.g. questions relating to colour if the system does not use colour, questions referring to printouts if there is no printer attached), then please write: **'Not applicable'** or **'N/A'** in the 'Comments' column beside that question, and move on to the next question.

(6) After the checklist questions in each section, you are asked for: **'... any comments (good or bad) ...'** which you would like to add concerning the issues in that section.

   For example, you may wish to describe a particular problem, or make a particular point which you did not have room to make beside the checklist question, or you may feel that the checklist questions have not covered a particular aspect of the interface which you feel should be mentioned.

(7) At the end of each section, you will see a rating scale, ranging from **'Very satisfactory'** to **'Very unsatisfactory'**. Please tick the box which best describes the way you feel about the user interface in terms of the issues in that section.

Section 10: system usability problems

(1) The questions in this section ask you about specific problems which you experienced when carrying out the evaluation task(s).

(2) To the right of each question you will see three columns labelled: **'No problems'**, **'Minor problems'** and **'Major problems'**.

   For each question, please tick the column which is most appropriate.

(3) As in Sections 1 to 9, please write any particular comments, descriptions of problems, and so on, in the column labelled **'Comments'**, beside each question.

(4) If there are any questions which you feel are not relevant to the interface which you are evaluating, then please write: **'Not applicable'** or **'N/A'** in the 'Comments' column for that question.

Section 11: general questions on system usability

This section asks you to give your views on the interface which you have been evaluating. Please feel free to write as much as you like in answer to each question.

SECTION 1: VISUAL CLARITY

Information displayed on the screen should be clear, well-organized, unambiguous and easy to read.

	Always	Most of the time	Some of the time	Never	Comments
1. Is each screen clearly identified with an informative title or description?					
2. Is important information highlighted on the screen? (e.g. cursor position, instructions, errors)					
3. When the user enters information on the screen, is it clear: (a) where the information should be entered?					
(b) in what format it should be entered?					
4. Where the user overtypes information on the screen, does the system clear the previous information, so that it does not get confused with the updated input?					
5. Does information appear to be organized logically on the screen? (e.g. menus organized by probable sequence of selection, or alphabetically)					
6. Are different types of information clearly separated from each other on the screen? (e.g. instructions, control options, data displays)					
7. Where a large amount of information is displayed on one screen, is it clearly separated into sections on the screen?					
8. Are columns of information clearly aligned on the screen? (e.g. columns of alphanumerics left-justified, columns of integers right-justified)					
9. Are bright or light colours displayed on a dark background, and vice versa?					
10. Does the use of colour help to make the displays clear?					
11. Where colour is used, will all aspects of the display be easy to see if used on a monochrome or low resolution screen, or if the user is colour-blind?					
12. Is the information on the screen easy to see and read?					

	Always	Most of the time	Some of the time	Never	Comments
13. Do screens appear uncluttered?					
14. Are schematic and pictorial displays (e.g. figures and diagrams) clearly drawn and annotated?					
15. Is it easy to find the required information on a screen?					

16. Are there any comments (good or bad) you wish to add regarding the above issues?

17. Overall, how would you rate the system in terms of visual clarity?
    (Please tick appropriate box below.)

Very satisfactory	Moderately satisfactory	Neutral	Moderately unsatisfactory	Very unsatisfactory

SECTION 2: CONSISTENCY

The way the system looks and works should be consistent at all times.

	Always	Most of the time	Some of the time	Never	Comments
1. Are different colours used consistently throughout the system? (e.g. errors always highlighted in the same colour)					
2. Are abbreviations, acronyms, codes and other alphanumeric information used consistently throughout the system?					
3. Are icons, symbols, graphical representations and other pictorial information used consistently throughout the system?					
4. Is the same type of information (e.g. instructions, menus, messages, titles) displayed: (a) in the same location on the screen?					

	Always	Most of the time	Some of the time	Never	Comments
(b) in the same layout?					
5. Does the cursor appear in the same initial position on displays of a similar type?					
6. Is the same item of information displayed in the same format, wherever it appears?					
7. Is the format in which the user should enter particular types of information on the screen consistent throughout the system?					
8. Is the method of entering information consistent throughout the system?					
9. Is the action required to move the cursor around the screen consistent throughout the system?					
10. Is the method of selecting options (e.g. from a menu) consistent throughout the system?					
11. Where a keyboard is used, are the same keys used for the same functions throughout the system?					
12. Are there standard procedures for carrying out similar, related operations? (e.g. updating and deleting information, starting and finishing transactions)					
13. Is the way the system responds to a particular user action consistent at all times?					

14. Are there any comments (good or bad) you wish to add regarding the above issues?

15. Overall, how would you rate the system in terms of consistency?
    (Please tick appropriate box below.)

Very satisfactory	Moderately satisfactory	Neutral	Moderately unsatisfactory	Very unsatisfactory

SECTION 3: COMPATIBILITY

The way the system looks and works should be compatible with user conventions and expectations.

	Always	Most of the time	Some of the time	Never	Comments
1. Are colours assigned according to conventional associations where these are important? (e.g. red = alarm, stop)					
2. Where abbreviations, acronyms, codes and other alphanumeric information are displayed: (a) are they easy to recognize and understand?					
(b) do they follow conventions where these exist?					
3. Where icons, symbols, graphical representations and other pictorial information are displayed: (a) are they easy to recognize and understand?					
(b) do they follow conventions where these exist?					
4. Where jargon and terminology is used within the system, is it familiar to the user?					
5. Are established conventions followed for the format in which particular types of information are displayed? (e.g. layout of dates and telephone numbers)					
6. Is information presented and analysed in the units with which the users normally work? (e.g. batches, kilos, dollars)					
7. Is the format of displayed information compatible with the form in which it is entered into the system?					
8. Is the format and sequence in which information is printed compatible with the way it is displayed on the screen?					
9. Where the user makes an input movement in a particular direction (e.g. using a direction key, mouse, or joystick), is the corresponding movement on the screen in the same direction?					
10. Are control actions compatible with those used in other systems with which the user may need to interact?					

	Always	Most of the time	Some of the time	Never	Comments
11. Is information presented in a way which fits the user's view of the task?					
12. Are graphical displays compatible with the user's view of what they are representing?					
13. Does the organization and structure of the system fit the user's perception of the task?					
14. Does the sequence of activities required to complete a task follow what the user would expect?					
15. Does the system work in the way the user thinks it should work?					

16. Are there any comments (good or bad) you wish to add regarding the above issues?

17. Overall, how would you rate the system in terms of compatibility?
    (Please tick appropriate box below.)

Very satisfactory	Moderately satisfactory	Neutral	Moderately unsatisfactory	Very unsatisfactory

SECTION 4: INFORMATIVE FEEDBACK

Users should be given clear, informative feedback on where they are in the system, what actions they have taken, whether these actions have been successful and what actions should be taken next.

	Always	Most of the time	Some of the time	Never	Comments
1. Are instructions and messages displayed by the system concise and positive?					

	Always	Most of the time	Some of the time	Never	Comments
2. Are messages displayed by the system relevant?					
3. Do instructions and prompts clearly indicate what to do?					
4. Is it clear what actions the user can take at any stage?					
5. Is it clear what the user needs to do in order to take a particular action? (e.g. which options to select, which keys to press)					
6. When the user enters information on the screen, is it made clear what this information should be?					
7. Is it made clear what shortcuts, if any, are possible? (e.g. abbreviations, hidden commands, type-ahead)					
8. Is it made clear what changes occur on the screen as a result of a user input or action?					
9. Is there always an appropriate system response to a user input or action?					
10. Are status messages (e.g. indicating what the system is doing, or has just done):					
(a) informative?					
(b) accurate?					
11. Does the system clearly inform the user when it completes a requested action (successfully or unsuccessfully)?					
12. Does the system promptly inform the user of any delay, making it clear that the user's input or request is being processed?					
13. Do error messages explain clearly:					
(a) where the errors are?					
(b) what the errors are?					
(c) why they have occurred?					
14. Is it clear to the user what should be done to correct an error?					
15. Where there are several modes of operation, does the system clearly indicate which mode the user is currently in? (e.g. update, enquiry, simulation)					

16. Are there any comments (good or bad) you wish to add regarding the above issues?

17. Overall, how would you rate the system in terms of informative feedback?
(Please tick appropriate box below.)

Very satisfactory	Moderately satisfactory	Neutral	Moderately unsatisfactory	Very unsatisfactory

SECTION 5: EXPLICITNESS

The way the system works and is structured should be clear to the user.

	Always	Most of the time	Some of the time	Never	Comments
1. Is it clear what stage the system has reached in a task?					
2. Is it clear what the user needs to do in order to complete a task?					
3. Where the user is presented with a list of options (e.g. in a menu), is it clear what each option means?					
4. Is it clear what part of the system the user is in?					
5. Is it clear what the different parts of the system do?					
6. Is it clear how, where and why changes in one part of the system affect other parts of the system?					
7. Is it clear why the system is organized and structured as it is?					
8. Is it clear why a series of screens are sequenced as they are?					
9. Is the structure of the system obvious to the user?					
10. Is the system well-organized from the user's point of view?					

	Always	Most of the time	Some of the time	Never	Comments
11. Where an interface metaphor is used (e.g. the desk-top metaphor in office applications), is this made explicit?					
12. Where a metaphor is employed, and is only applicable to certain parts of the system, is this made explicit?					
13. In general, is it clear what the system is doing?					

14. Are there any comments (good or bad) you wish to add regarding the above issues?

15. Overall, how would you rate the system in terms of explicitness?
(Please tick appropriate box below.)

Very satisfactory	Moderately satisfactory	Neutral	Moderately unsatisfactory	Very unsatisfactory

SECTION 6: APPROPRIATE FUNCTIONALITY

The system should meet the needs and requirements of users when carrying out tasks.

	Always	Most of the time	Some of the time	Never	Comments
1. Is the input device available to the user (e.g. pointing device, keyboard, joystick) appropriate for the tasks to be carried out?					
2. Is the way in which information is presented appropriate for the tasks?					
3. Does each screen contain all the information which the user feels is relevant to the task?					
4. Are users provided with all the options which they feel are necessary at any particular stage in a task?					
5. Can users access all the information which they feel they need for their current task?					

	Always	Most of the time	Some of the time	Never	Comments
6. Does the system allow users to do what they feel is necessary in order to carry out a task?					
7. Is system feedback appropriate for the task?					
8. Do the contents of help and tutorial facilities make use of realistic task data and problems?					
9. Is task-specific jargon and terminology defined at an early stage in the task?					
10. Where interface metaphors are used, are they relevant to the tasks carried out using the system?					
11. Where task sequences are particularly long, are they broken into appropriate subsequences? (e.g. separating a lengthy editing procedure into its constituent parts)					

12. Are there any comments (good or bad) you wish to add regarding the above issues?

13. Overall, how would you rate the system in terms of appropriate functionality? (Please tick appropriate box below.)

Very satisfactory	Moderately satisfactory	Neutral	Moderately unsatisfactory	Very unsatisfactory

SECTION 7: FLEXIBILITY AND CONTROL

The interface should be sufficiently flexible in structure, in the way information is presented and in terms of what the user can do, to suit the needs and requirements of all users, and to allow them to feel in control of the system.

	Always	Most of the time	Some of the time	Never	Comments
1. Is there an easy way for the user to 'undo' an action, and step back to a previous stage or screen? (e.g. if the user makes a wrong choice, or does something unintended)					

	Always	Most of the time	Some of the time	Never	Comments
2. Where the user can 'undo', is it possible to 'redo' (i.e. to reverse this action)?					
3. Are shortcuts available when required? (e.g. to bypass a sequence of activities or screens)					
4. Do users have control over the order in which they request information, or carry out a series of activities?					
5. Can the user look through a sequence of screens in either direction?					
6. Can the user access a particular screen in a sequence of screens directly? (e.g. where a list or table covers several screens)					
7. In menu-based systems, is it easy to return to the main menu from any part of the system?					
8. Can the user move to different parts of the system as required?					
9. Is the user able to finish entering information (e.g. when typing in a list or table of information) before the system responds? (e.g. by updating the screen)					
10. Does the system prefill repeated information on the screen, where possible? (e.g. to save the user having to enter the same information several times)					
11. Can the user choose whether to enter information manually or to let the computer generate information automatically? (e.g. where there are defaults)					
12. Can the user override computer-generated (e.g. default) information, if appropriate?					
13. Can the user choose the rate at which information is presented?					
14. Can the user choose how to name and organize information which may need to be recalled at a later stage? (e.g. files, directories)					
15. Can users tailor certain aspects of the interface for their own preferences or needs? (e.g. colours, parameters)					

16. Are there any comments (good or bad) you wish to add regarding the above issues?

17. Overall, how would you rate the system in terms of flexibility and control?
(Please tick appropriate box below.)

Very satisfactory	Moderately satisfactory	Neutral	Moderately unsatisfactory	Very unsatisfactory

SECTION 8: ERROR PREVENTION AND CORRECTION

The system should be designed to minimize the possibility of user error, with inbuilt facilities for detecting and handling those which do occur; users should be able to check their inputs and to correct errors, or potential error situations before the input is processed.

	Always	Most of the time	Some of the time	Never	Comments
1. Does the system validate user inputs before processing, wherever possible?					
2. Does the system clearly and promptly inform the user when it detects an error?					
3. Does the system inform the user when the amount of information entered exceeds the available space? (e.g. trying to key five digits into a four-digit field)					
4. Are users able to check what they have entered before it is processed?					
5. Is there some form of cancel (or 'undo') key for the user to reverse an error situation?					
6. Is it easy for the user to correct errors?					
7. Does the system ensure that the user corrects all detected errors before the input is processed?					
8. Can the user try out possible actions (e.g. using a simulation facility) without the system processing the input and causing problems?					
9. Is the system protected against common trivial errors?					

	Always	Most of the time	Some of the time	Never	Comments
10. Does the system ensure that the user double-checks any requested actions which may be catastrophic if requested unintentionally? (e.g. large-scale deletion)					
11. Is the system protected against possible knock-on effects of changes in one part of the system?					
12. Does the system prevent users from taking actions which they are not authorized to take? (e.g. by requiring passwords)					
13. In general, is the system free from errors and malfunctions?					
14. When system errors occur, can the user access all necessary diagnostic information to resolve the problem (e.g. where and what the fault is, what is required to resolve it)					

15. Are there any comments (good or bad) you wish to add regarding the above issues?

16. Overall, how would you rate the system in terms of error prevention and correction?
                        (Please tick appropriate box below.)

Very satisfactory	Moderately satisfactory	Neutral	Moderately unsatisfactory	Very unsatisfactory

SECTION 9: USER GUIDANCE AND SUPPORT

Informative, easy-to-use and relevant guidance and support should be provided, both on the computer (via an on-line help facility) and in hard-copy document form, to help the user understand and use the system.

	Always	Most of the time	Some of the time	Never	Comments
1. If there is some form of help facility (or guidance) on the computer to help the user when using the system then: (a) Can the user request this easily from any point in the system?					
(b) Is it clear how to get in and out of the help facility?					
(c) Is the help information presented clearly, without interfering with the user's current activity?					
(d) When the user requests help, does the system clearly explain the possible actions which can be taken, in the context of what the user is currently doing?					
(e) When using the help facility, can the user find relevant information directly, without having to look through unnecessary information?					
(f) Does the help facility allow the user to browse through information about other parts of the system?					
2. If there is some form of hard-copy guide to the system (e.g. user guide or manual) then: (a) Does this provide an in-depth, comprehensive description, covering all aspects of the system?					
(b) Is it easy to find the required section in the hard-copy documentation?					
3. Is the organization of all forms of user guidance and support related to the tasks which the user can carry out?					
4. Do user guidance and support facilities adequately explain both user and system errors, and how these should be corrected?					
5. Are all forms of user guidance and support maintained up-to-date?					

6. Are there any comments (good or bad) you wish to add regarding the above issues?

7. Overall, how would you rate the system in terms of user guidance and support?
(Please tick appropriate box below.)

Very satisfactory	Moderately satisfactory	Neutral	Moderately unsatisfactory	Very unsatisfactory

SECTION 10: SYSTEM USABILITY PROBLEMS

When using the system, did you experience problems with any of the following:

	No problems	Minor problems	Major problems	Comments
1. Working out how to use the system				
2. Lack of guidance on how to use the system				
3. Poor system documentation				
4. Understanding how to carry out the tasks				
5. Knowing what to do next				
6. Understanding how the information on the screen relates to what you are doing				
7. Finding the information you want				
8. Information which is difficult to read clearly				
9. Too many colours on the screen				
10. Colours which are difficult to look at for any length of time				
11. An inflexible, rigid system structure				
12. An inflexible HELP (guidance) facility				
13. Losing track of where you are in the system or of what you are doing or have done				
14. Having to remember too much information while carrying out a task				
15. System response times that are too quick for you to understand what is going on				
16. Information which does not stay on the screen long enough for you to read it				

	No problems	Minor problems	Major problems	Comments
17. System response times that are too slow				
18. Unexpected actions by the system				
19. An input device which is difficult or awkward to use				
20. Knowing where or how to input information				
21. Having to spend too much time inputting information				
22. Having to be very careful in order to avoid errors				
23. Working out how to correct errors				
24. Having to spend too much time correcting errors				
25. Having to carry out the same type of activity in different ways				

SECTION 11: GENERAL QUESTIONS ON SYSTEM USABILITY

Please give your views on the usability of the system by answering the questions below in the spaces provided. There are no right or wrong answers.

1. What are the best aspects of the system for the user?

2. What are the worst aspects of the system for the user?

3. Are there any parts of the system which you found confusing or difficult to fully understand?

4. Were there any aspects of the system which you found particularly irritating although they did not cause major problems?

5. What were the most common mistakes you made when using the system?

6. What changes would you make to the system to make it better from the user's point of view?

7. Is there anything else about the system you would like to add?

4

Detailed explanations of criterion-based sections

4.1 CHECKLIST SECTION 1: VISUAL CLARITY

Information displayed on the screen should be clear, well-organized, unambiguous and easy to read.

4.1.1 Description of visual clarity

This concerns the way in which information is displayed on the screen. Good visual clarity should:

— make the screen appear uncluttered;
— enable the user to find required information and to see where information should be entered on the screen, quickly and easily;
— draw the user's attention to important information;
— enable users to see and read information on the screen clearly and easily.

Although the amount of information displayed should be kept to a minimum as far as possible, complex displays are often necessary, and can easily appear cluttered if poorly designed. This may lengthen the time taken by the user to find information on the screen and can lead to misinterpretation and errors. Users may feel that the display is too complex for them to understand, or that they have not got time to try to understand it (Galitz, 1980). Highly detailed displays should be organized and structured to avoid unnecessary complexity, with information grouped in meaningful ways rather than in random patterns (Galitz, 1980).

4.1.2   Explanation of visual clarity checklist questions
Question 1. Is each screen clearly identified with an informative title or description?

A relevant and informative title or description, clearly located and presented on the screen, provides the user with an explanation of what is being displayed.

Question 2. Is important information highlighted on the screen? (e.g. cursor position, instructions, errors)

Techniques such as increased brightness, the use of different colours, reverse video and flashing, for instance, can help to draw the user's attention to important information on the screen. Care should be taken when choosing how to highlight particular information. Certain techniques may be too obtrusive or distracting when using the system (e.g. bright flashing), while others may not be obvious enough (e.g. a different colour when the screen already contains a number of colours). Similarly, while certain information is obviously important in any context (e.g. error messages, position of the cursor), the necessity to highlight other information may only be revealed when actually using the interface to carry out a task (e.g. in an evaluation).

Question 3. When the user enters information on the screen, is it clear where, and in what format, it should be entered?

Both speed and efficiency of interaction will be increased if users can see where they should enter information on the screen, and if the format in which this information should be entered is obvious to them. Highlighting the cursor (see question 2 above) draws the user's attention to the relevant location. Clear instructions, consistency, compatibility and an explicit on-line help facility can all help the user to identify the format in which information should be entered. In addition, the required format can be indicated by techniques such as marking the entry field on the screen (e.g. '../../..').

Question 4. Where the user overtypes information on the screen, does the system clear the previous information, so that it does not get confused with the updated input?

This is extremely important in order to avoid confusion and error. Typing over existing information can be confusing, and users may forget to delete the information which they are overtyping. For example, an existing item of information may read: '100'. If the user replaces this with '20' and forgets to delete the existing figure, then the resulting figure will read '200', which is obviously incorrect.

Question 5. Does information appear to be organised logically on the screen? (e.g. menus organized by probable sequence of selection, or alphabetically)

If the location, layout and order in which information is displayed appears to be logical to users, then they are likely to find required information more quickly. Similarly, users may find it easier to understand what the screen is displaying, if information is organized in a way which makes sense to them.

Question 6. Are different types of information clearly separated from each other on the screen? (e.g. instructions, control options, data displays)

It is important for the user to be able to identify different types of information on the screen quickly and without difficulty. If these are not separated in some way, then they may appear to 'merge' on the screen, causing confusion and the appearance of clutter. The user may find it difficult to see where, for example, instructions begin and end. It may also be more difficult for the user to locate required information on the screen.

Question 7. Where a large amount of information is displayed on one screen, is it clearly separated into sections on the screen?

Where a large amount of information is displayed on the screen, there may be a need for more separations than just those between different types of information (as described in question 6 above). Without this, a full screen can appear cluttered and confusing, even if information is organized logically. For example, a large table of data, spreading across and down the screen could be split horizontally after every five or so items by inserting a blank line.

Question 8. Are columns of information clearly aligned on the screen? (e.g. columns of alphanumerics left-justified, columns of integers right-justified)

In order to enhance the clarity of the display, columns of information must be clearly aligned.

Question 9. Are bright or light colours displayed on a dark background, and vice versa?

Where colours are used, it is much easier to see and read information on the screen where foreground and background differ significantly. For example, dark blue lettering on a white background will be easier to read than pale yellow lettering on the same background. Some people may have specific difficulty with particular colours, or colour combinations. It is extremely important that these are taken into account where users are likely to spend lengthy periods of time looking at the screen.

Question 10. Does the use of colour help to make the displays clear?
Effective use of colour can greatly enhance visual clarity, especially for those unfamilar with the screens. It can draw attention to different parts of the screen and can serve to highlight important information, and to separate different types of information. Poorly used, however, (e.g. insufficient contrast between background and text, colours which are too bright, too many colours on the screen), colour can make a screen extremely confusing, difficult to read, and unpleasant to look at. As mentioned above, people have different preferences for, and difficulties with, colour and this should be taken into account.

Question 11. Where colour is used, will all aspects of the display be easy to see if used on a monochrome or low resolution screen, or if the user is colour-blind?
When considering the use of colour on the screen, it is important to investigate whether colour-blind people can read the screens easily. If the interface may rely on a monochrome screen, then this should also be carefully examined.

Question 12. Is information on the screen easy to see and read?
This relates not only to factors covered in other questions in this section, such as use of colour and organization of information on the screen, but also to aspects such as screen resolution and quality and size of characters on the screen. It is important to ensure that visual differences are accommodated as far as possible, so that information will be visually clear and readable to all who use the system.

Question 13. Do screens appear uncluttered?
This relates closely to the rest of this section, and in particular to questions 6, 7 and 8, since good organization of information on the screen can help to avoid the appearance of clutter. However, there may be occasions, for example, where a screen appears cluttered, regardless of how well organized it is, because it simply contains too much information.

Question 14. Are schematic and pictorial displays (e.g. figures and diagrams) clearly drawn and annotated?
The annotation and labelling of graphs, figures, diagrams, etc., has important implications for the user's ability to understand and respond to the presented information.

Question 15. Is it easy to find the required information on a screen?
This question provides an overall assessment of visual clarity, as the above questions primarily aim to enable users to find the information they require, quickly and easily. If, however, an evaluator answers the above questions positively, but has difficulty finding required information, then it is likely that there is a problem with one of the other criteria (e.g. poor consistency or compatibility, lack of informative feedback or user guidance). The reverse may be true if, for example, the above questions are answered negatively, but information is easy to find.

4.2   CHECKLIST SECTION 2: CONSISTENCY
The way the system looks and works should be consistent at all times.

4.2.1   Description of consistency
Consistency is concerned with creating and reinforcing user expectations by maintaining predictability across the interface.

   If users can predict what the system will do, or what information will appear when and where, then:

— they can learn more quickly and effectively;
— their confusion is reduced as they are not surprised by unexpected system actions or displays;
— their search and response times are likely to be reduced;
— they know where to look in order to find particular information;
— they know where important information will appear;
— they can be more effective and efficient when inputting information, as they learn quickly what actions are required of them, and can generalize these across the rest of the system;
— working memory load is reduced, as they do not have to remember very different actions for every different part of the system;
— they are less likely to make errors.

   In summary, consistency can greatly increase speed of learning, improve efficiency and effectiveness of human–computer interaction, and significantly reduce the likelihood of errors.

4.2.2   Explanation of consistency checklist questions

Question 1. Are different colours used consistently throughout the system? (e.g. errors always highlighted in the same colour)
People naturally tend to use colour as a means of initial recognition and identification. For example, if a warning message is coloured red on one screen, then users may assume that all warning messages will be coloured red. If on a future occasion, a warning is displayed in green, the user may not recognize the message as being a warning, and this could cause problems. Changing the use of colour through the interface, can cause confusion, errors and misinterpretation.

Question 2. Are abbreviations, acronyms, codes and other alphanumeric information used consistently throughout the system?
Consistency here can greatly increase speed of learning and recognition.

Question 3. Are icons, symbols, graphical representations and other pictorial information used consistently throughout the system?
As with colours, it is important that pictorial representations are used consistently, so that users can learn to recognize them quickly and accurately.

Question 4. Is the same type of information (e.g. instructions, menus, messages, titles) displayed in the same location on the screen and in the same layout?
This helps the user to learn where to look for particular information on the screen, and to recognize, interpret and respond to the information quickly.

Question 5. Does the cursor appear in the same initial position on displays of a similar type?
This saves the user having to search the screen for the cursor, when a screen is initially displayed.

Question 6. Is the same item of information displayed in the same format, wherever it appears?
This assists the user in recognizing specific items of information on the screen. Inconsistent format of information may mean that the user has difficulty in recognizing the item of information as being the same as previously encountered. This may slow search and learning time.

Question 7. Is the format in which the user should enter particular types of information on the screen consistent throughout the system?
Where the user enters information which can appear in a number of formats (e.g. dates), it is extremely important that the required format is always the same. This helps to avoid errors, which can occur if the user has to learn and remember different formats on different occasions, and increases speed both of learning and of information entry by the user.

Question 8. Is the method of entering information consistent throughout the system?
A user entering a number of items of information on the same screen, for example, may have to press 'return' after each item, before entering the next item. Alternatively, the cursor may move automatically to the next item, or the user may be able to move the cursor using a direction key or mouse, and need only press 'return' after entering all the information for that particular screen. One method of input should be used as an internal standard throughout the system.

Question 9. Is the action required to move the cursor around the screen consistent throughout the system?
For instance, if the cursor is moved by pressing direction keys on one screen, then direction keys should be used on all screens. This helps learning and speed of interaction and avoids user frustration if the user does not have to remember different actions for different screens. If the user has several options available for cursor movement (e.g. direction keys and mouse), then the same options should be available at all times.

Question 10. Is the method of selecting options (e.g. from a menu) consistent throughout the system?
For example, a menu option may be selected by moving the cursor down a list with a direction key or a mouse, and pressing 'return' on reaching the option. As above, one method should be used consistently.

Question 11. Where a keyboard is used, are the same keys used for the same functions throughout the system?
Again, this assists the user in learning how to use the system. It also increases speed of interaction, and reduces errors, as the user does not have to remember different control actions in different parts of the system.

***Question 12. Are there standard procedures for carrying out
similar, related operations? (e.g. updating and deleting information,
starting and finishing transactions)***
Similar operation sequences, such as updating and deleting information, should require a similar set of actions. Again, this saves the
user extra learning, avoids errors and increases speed of interaction.

***Question 13. Is the way the system responds to a particular user
action, consistent at all times?***
This helps to build predictability into the system. If the system
responds in different ways at different times to the same type of user
actions, then users may become confused and frustrated, and may
wonder if they have made an error. If the system always responds in
the same way to the same user action, then the user should quickly
notice response changes, and will therefore be alerted to any
problem. Similarly, if the system always responds in the same way
when the user makes a mistake, then the user will recognize errors
quickly.

4.3   CHECKLIST SECTION 3: COMPATIBILITY

The way the system looks and works should be compatible with user
conventions and expectations.

4.3.1   Description of compatibility
Compatibility is concerned with ensuring that the interface conforms
with existing user expectations, where appropriate. If the interface is
compatible with these expectations, then it should be easy for users to
recognize aspects of the interface without difficulty, understand and
interpret what they are looking at and what the system is doing, and
easily identify what actions to take.

Likely sources of these expectations are conventions existing
within the general population, or 'population stereotypes' (e.g. in
Europe, dates are commonly sequenced 'dd/mm/yy'; the colour 'red'
generally indicates 'danger' or 'stop'); conventions specific to a
particular user population (e.g. specific terminology used; specific
units in which information is measured); previous experience with
other computer applications, affecting what users expect to see and
do (i.e. the user's mental representation, or 'cognitive model', of the
interface and the system).

Some caution should be noted, however. For example, in certain
cases it may be more appropriate to introduce new aspects into the

interface, and to familiarize users with these by consistency, comprehensive guidance and support and informative feedback. An additional caution should be noted when considering compatibility with user expectations arising from their understanding of the application. In some situations, user assumptions may actually be based on misperceptions or misunderstanding. Care should be taken to ensure that these are identified and overcome (e.g. with more appropriate and explicit feedback, guidance and support).

4.3.2   Explanation of compatibility checklist questions

Question 1. Are colours assigned according to conventional associations where these are important? (e.g. red = alarm, stop)
People naturally make associations with particular colours. Certain colours have very definite meanings within populations. Retaining important associations (such as red for errors or emergencies), makes the user's task of understanding presented information much easier than if conventional associations are not followed.

Question 2. Where abbreviations, acronyms, codes and other alphanumeric information are displayed, are they easy to recognize and understand, and do they follow conventions where these exist?
Conventions may be specific to a particular user group, or may be general to the population as a whole. They may also be specific to the particular tasks which the system is to carry out. End-users should be consulted, where possible, to ensure that any such conventions are followed. Where these do not exist, then any alphanumeric representations should be as clear and unambiguous as possible.

Question 3. Where icons, symbols, graphical representations and other pictorial information are displayed, are they easy to recognize and understand, and do they follow conventions where these exist?
As in question 2 above, conventions should be followed as far as possible. However, where these do not exist, it is essential that any pictorial information can be recognized and intepreted without difficulty.

Question 4. Where jargon and terminology is used within the system, is it familiar to the user?
The terminology and jargon which the system adopts should be familiar to the user, in order to avoid unnecessary confusions.

Question 5. Are established conventions followed for the format in which particular types of information are displayed? (e.g. layout of dates and telephone numbers)

As above, end-users should be consulted with respect to any conventions specific to the context within which the system is to be used. The interface should also follow any more general population stereotypes which may exist.

Question 6. Is information presented and analysed in the units with which the users normally work? (e.g. batches, kilos, dollars)

This is important in order to avoid disruption of the user's work, as information is likely to be presented and analysed in the same units wherever it is used. If the interface is to be used within different environments, which may use different units of analysis, then different options should be available.

Question 7. Is the format of displayed information compatible with the form in which it is entered into the system?

If, for example, a date in displayed on the screen in the sequence 'dd/mm/yy', then any date entered on the screen by the user should be sequenced in the same way. This makes it easier for users to recognize the item displayed on the screen as being the item which they entered into the system. It also makes it easier for the user to identify the format in which an item of information should be entered.

Question 8. Is the format and sequence in which information is printed compatible with the way it is displayed on the screen?

If users request certain information to be printed, while carrying out a task using the computer application, then it is important that they can reference the printed material to the screen from which it was requested.

Question 9. Where the user makes an input movement in a particular direction (e.g. using a direction key, mouse, or joystick), is the corresponding movement on the screen in the same direction?

This helps to avoid user confusion and errors by enhancing control–display compatibility.

Question 10. Are control actions compatible with those used in other systems with which the user may need to interact?

As with consistency of control actions across screens, this aims to ensure that the user can transfer experience as far as possible, instead of having to learn different actions for new systems.

Question 11. Is information presented in a way which fits the user's view of the task?

Users are likely to have a better understanding of what they are looking at, and of how this relate to what they are trying to do, if information is presented on the screen as they would expect to see it in the context of the task. This reduces confusion which may arise if users find it difficult to relate what they see to what they expect. It therefore facilitates learning, and increases the speed with which users are able to locate required information on the screen. This is often referred to as 'cognitive compatibility'.

Question 12. Are graphical displays compatible with the user's view of what they are representing?

If users can identify immediately and without difficulty how a graphical display relates to what it is representing, then this can provide a rapid and effective means of presenting information. If not, however, then the display may appear confusing, and users may find it difficult to understand the presented information.

Question 13. Does the organization and structure of the system fit the user's perception of the task?

This concerns the structure of different parts of the system, and how these interrelate. For example, the user may perceive a number of task-related activities to be independent from each other, and may therefore expect these to fall within different parts of the system (e.g. within different 'branches' of the system). Equally, users may perceive other activities as being highly interrelated, and might expect these to be included in the same part of the system (e.g. accessible from the same menu). If a group of activities or steps are likely to be carried out in a particular sequence, then the user may expect the organization of these within the system to follow that sequence. When a user is unfamiliar with the task, a well-organized system which 'maps logically' onto the task, can help the user to develop an accurate 'mental representation' of the task, and of what it involves.

Question 14. Does the sequence of activities required to complete a task follow what the user would expect?

Users can become frustrated and confused if they are not able to carry out the activities required to complete a task in the sequence which they expect; they may lose track of what they are doing, of what stage they have reached in the task, and of what to do next. If, for some reason, it is not feasible or appropriate for the system to follow the sequence of activities expected by the user (e.g. where users currently carry out the task manually, and expect the manual process to be transferred to the computer exactly), then comprehensive feedback, instructions and user guidance can help users to learn the required sequence.

Question 15. Does the system work in the way the user thinks it should work?
Although this question overlaps to some extent with the above four questions, it is extremely important as a means of identifying the user's overall perception of the interface and of the system as a whole. It may enable an assessment of whether the user has a misconception of the task, of the interface, or of the system.

4.4   CHECKLIST SECTION 4: INFORMATIVE FEEDBACK

Users should be given clear, informative feedback on where they are in the system, what actions they have taken, whether these actions have been successful and what actions should be taken next.

4.4.1   Description of informative feedback
Informative feedback is extremely important for users, both when learning how the interface works and how to use it, and in understanding what the system is doing and what the user can do at any particular stage of the task. It provides users with information about the system, in the context of the task being carried out, including what has just happened, what is currently happening, and what can, should or will happen next.

This helps to promote users' understanding of how the system works and is structured. It is essential that the user builds an accurate mental representation of the interface, in order to avoid misconceptions, misunderstandings and confusion. The quality and timing of feedback is therefore extremely important. Messages and instructions should not only be clear, concise, positive and easy to understand, but they should be displayed when appropriate, and their content should be relevant to the current situation.

Caution should be exercised when considering the amount of feedback to provide. Too much feedback can overload the user and clutter the screen. The optimum amount of feedback in any situation may depend on the level of experience of the users. Novice users are likely to require more feedback than those with more experience, and the amount of feedback which is suitable for a novice may be extremely irritating to a more experienced user. Extra instructions and information which may be required for novices could be covered by a comprehensive tutorial program, by an on-line 'help' facility (see Section 9) and, where appropriate, by some form of hard-copy user guide. However, where an application is to be used mainly by novice users (e.g. where users are unlikely to use the system frequently enough to become experienced) then extra feedback may be required.

4.4.2   Explanation of informative feedback checklist questions

Question 1. Are instructions and messages displayed by the system concise and positive?
It is important that information presented in the form of instructions and messages is concise and to the point. This not only saves the user from having to read through unnecessary material, but it also enables the user to take in the information more quickly and accurately. The language used should be phrased positively, indicating what to do, rather than what to avoid, for example.

Question 2. Are messages displayed by the system relevant?
Whether messages which the system displays are relevant or not will depend on the context within which they are displayed.

Question 3. Do instructions and prompts clearly indicate what to do?
These can be vital in assisting a user in learning how to use the system, in understanding what is happening, and in actually using the system. It is extremely important that the appropriate amount of instruction and prompting is provided, and that the language used is appropriate for the end-users.

Question 4. Is it clear what actions the user can take at any stage?
Clear instructions and prompts, together with context-sensitive on-line 'help' (see Section 9), are all important here.

Question 5. Is it clear what the user needs to do in order to take a particular action? (e.g. which options to select, which keys to press)
Again, instructions and prompts, and user guidance play an important role here.

Question 6. When the user enters information on the screen, is it made clear what this information should be?

Clear instructions, a good on-line 'help' facility and good system documentation can all assist in clarifying what information the user should enter.

Question 7. Is it made clear what shortcuts, if any, are possible? (e.g. abbreviations, hidden commands, type-ahead)

This question is not concerned with whether any shortcuts exist, but with whether the feedback is sufficient for the user to know whether there are any, and if so, what they are.

Question 8. Is it made clear what changes occur on the screen as a result of a user input or action?

For example, the screen may be updated before the user has realized what has happened, and it may then be hard to see what has changed. Good, clear, prompt system messages help to indicate what has changed, as can visual clarity (e.g. by highlighting the updated information).

Question 9. Is there always an appropriate system response to a user input or action?

It is essential that users receive appropriate acknowledgement from the system to any input or action, otherwise they may begin to doubt what they have done.

Question 10. Are status messages (e.g. indicating what the system is doing, or has just done) informative and accurate?

Status messages can be particularly valuable in reassuring the user when the computer is taking time to carry out a lengthy process. They should provide information which is not only accurate, but which is meaningful to the user in the context of the task. For example, a status message which explains, in computer jargon, a technical process which the computer is currently carrying out (e.g. 'writing data to temporary storage') may be of little value to the user, and is likely to cause confusion.

Question 11. Does the system clearly inform the user when it completes a requested action (successfully or unsuccessfully)?

The system should not only acknowledge any actions made by the user, but should also inform the user of the completion and success (or otherwise) of any actions which it has taken. This relates to a large extent to the frequency and adequacy of status messages (question 10 above).

Question 12. Does the system promptly inform the user of any delay, making it clear that the user's input or request is being processed?
Status messages are important here (see question 10 above), particularly with respect to lengthy system response times.

Question 13. Do error messages explain clearly where and what the errors are, and why they have occurred?
A message which reads 'Error', followed by a meaningless error code, which requires users to refer to a manual in order to determine what they have done wrong, is not sufficient. It is important to inform users not only that they have made an error, but also of where and what the error is, and why it is an error. For example, a message might indicate that the user has made a syntax error (i.e. 'what' the error is), on line 12 (i.e. 'where' the error is), because there is an extra, unpaired, bracket (i.e. 'why' it is an error).

Question 14. Is it clear to the user what should be done to correct an error?
Where possible, error messages should clearly explain what should be done to correct an error.

Question 15. Where there are several modes of operation, does the system clearly indicate which mode the user is currently in? (e.g. update, enquiry, simulation).
This is extremely important to user performance, as many common errors using contemporary interfaces are those termed 'mode' errors.

4.5   CHECKLIST SECTION 5: EXPLICITNESS

The way the system works and is structured should be clear to the user.

4.5.1   Description of explicitness
The main aim of this criterion is to promote the circumstances in which the user can develop a clear and accurate understanding of the interface, of how it is structured, what it does, and how it relates to the application tasks. Explicitness helps to make the interface 'transparent' to the user. If this is achieved, then the user is more likely to develop a clear and accurate mental representation of the interface,

and may therefore be able to use the interface and complete tasks more successfully, with greater ease.

The criteria described so far have a considerable influence on explicitness of the interface. Failure of the interface to meet any one of them is likely to have a negative effect on explictness. Similarly, if the interface is organized in a logical, straightforward way, appropriate for the application tasks, then the need for excessive feedback and user guidance may be slightly reduced.

4.5.2 Explanation of explicitness checklist questions

Question 1: Is it clear what stage the system has reached in a task?
Provision of informative feedback by the system is extremely important here, and context-sensitive on-line 'help' can be of great benefit. This question also tests how compatible the structure and functioning of the system is with the user's perception of the task (see Section 3).

Question 2. Is it clear what the user needs to do in order to complete a task?
As above, informative feedback is extremely important here, as is compatibility. Context-sensitive on-line 'help' and a comprehensive user guide or manual (see Section 9) are also relevant.

Question 3. Where the user is presented with a list of options (e.g. in a menu), is it clear what each option means?
The meaning of all options which are presented to the user, whether in a menu or otherwise, should be sufficiently clear that the user can easily decide which option is required next.

Question 4. Is it clear what part of the system the user is in?
Clear headings on every screen (see Section 1, question 1), comprehensive feedback, and clearly and logically organized menus, icons and command languages are extremely important here. The mode within which the user is to carry out tasks must be made explicit.

Question 5. Is it clear what the different parts of the system do?
In addition to the points made in question 4, comprehensive and well-organized hard-copy system documentation and an on-line 'help' facility which allows the user to browse through different sections (see Section 9), can also influence this.

Question 6. Is it clear how, where and why changes in one part of the system affect other parts of the system?
This is influenced by the same factors as question 4 above. It can help to reveal the user's view, or conceptual model, of the system.

Question 7. Is it clear why the system is organized and structured as it is?
The structure of the system may be obvious to the user, but it may be hard to identify why it has been organized in this way; in other words, it may be difficult to work out the designer's logic, especially in terms of the tasks. This would mean that users could find it harder to use the system efficiently than if the structure made logical sense to them.

Question 8. Is it clear why a series of screens are sequenced as they are?
It must be apparent to the user why screens are sequenced in a particular way, in order to foster a clearer understanding of the system's overall structure.

Question 9. Is the structure of the system obvious to the user?
A 'map' of the system structure can be a great help here, as can clear and well-organized system documentation, providing the user with an overview of the system.

Question 10. Is the system well-organized from the user's point of view?
Users may be able to see clearly why the system is structured as it is, but this may not seem particularly optimal, or even logical to them. If users cannot understand why the system is organized as it is (and therefore answer negatively to questions 7 and 8), then it is likely that they will answer this question negatively.

Question 11. Where an interface metaphor is used (e.g. the desk-top metaphor in office applications), is this made explicit?
For a user to benefit fully from the use of a metaphor in the interface's design, it is essential that this metaphor is made explicit and obvious to the user.

Question 12. Where a metaphor is employed, and is only applicable to certain parts of the system, is this made explicit?
In many cases, a metaphor that has been used to enhance the interaction cannot be extended to all parts of the system. In such cases, it is extremely important that these areas are clearly delineated

from those in which the metaphor is used. It is therefore necessary to make the limitations of the metaphor's application within the interface explicit.

Question 13. In general, is it clear what the system is doing?
This question reflects the adequacy of informative feedback provided by the system.

4.6 CHECKLIST SECTION 6: APPROPRIATE FUNCTIONALITY

The system should meet the needs and requirements of users when carrying out tasks.

4.6.1 Description of appropriate functionality
This concerns the user's perceived requirements of the interface when carrying out the task. If the interface does not provide users with the information, facilities, or options which they feel they require in order to carry out a task, then they may experience difficulty and frustration, and their efficiency when using the interface may be impaired.

It is particularly important to consult those with practical experience in the application domain, as their knowledge of what is required may be invaluable.

4.6.2 Explanation of appropriate functionality checklist questions

Question 1. Is the input device available to the user (e.g. pointing device, keyboard, joystick) appropriate for the tasks to be carried out?
For example, use of a mouse for pointing to objects on a screen may be considered an appropriate means of carrying out such an action.

Question 2. Is the way in which information is presented appropriate for the tasks.
For example, information defining a designed part may be most appropriately displayed as a dimensioned drawing, as opposed to listings of co-ordinates.

Question 3. Does each screen contain all the information which the user feels is relevant to the task?
Each screen should provide all information which the user requires at that stage of the task.

Question 4. Are users provided with all the options which they feel are necessary at any particular stage in a task?
When using the system, the user must feel that any desired action is represented as an option within the interface and that this option is available when required.

Question 5. Can users access all the information which they feel they need for their current task?
There may be occasions when users wish to refer to information other than that directly relevant while carrying out the task. This may be information held within a different database, for example. Users should be able to access such information, where possible.

Question 6. Does the system allow users to do what they feel is necessary in order to carry out a task?
This depends to a certain extent on the user's perception of the task. An experienced user's understanding of the task requirements will be based on practical experience. Those designing the interface should ensure that such experience is incorporated into the design.

Question 7. Is system feedback appropriate for the task?
This question relates to the various forms of feedback that the system offers (help, error messages, etc.), and its appropriateness in a realistic task context. If feedback is not relevant to what the user is currently doing, then this can be frustrating and misleading.

Question 8. Do the contents of help and tutorial facilities make use of realistic task data and problems?
It is especially important that users who are assisted, or 'taught', are exposed to material with which they are familiar within a task-related context. In addition, this material should approximate that which they will encounter when using the system.

Question 9. Is task-specific jargon and terminology defined at an early stage in the task?
It is important that users are introduced to terminology and jargon associated with the task at an early stage, so that later misunderstandings and confusion can be avoided.

Question 10. Where interface metaphors are used, are they relevant to the tasks carried out using the system?
Any metaphors employed by an interface should match the type of work for which the system is used. The use of metaphors can greatly

enhance the effectiveness of the user's interaction with a system, by promoting a particular view (or model) of the system which the user can understand easily. However, metaphors should always be used with great care, and it is important that they relate to the task as far as possible.

Question 11. Where task sequences are particularly long, are they broken into appropriate subsequences? (e.g. separating a lengthy editing procedure into its constituent parts)
For long task sequences, the demand placed on users' mental workload and working memory will be reduced if the sequences are divided into appropriate 'chunks' or subsequences.

4.7 CHECKLIST SECTION 7: FLEXIBILITY AND CONTROL

The interface should be sufficiently flexible in structure, in the way information is presented and in terms of what the user can do, to suit the needs and requirements of all users, and to allow them to feel in control of the system.

4.7.1 Description of flexibility and control
Flexibility aims to accommodate the needs and requirements of different users in different situations. It can help to increase speed and efficiency of interaction, and to reduce frustration. For example, it can reduce time-consuming activities such as repeated typing by the user of the same information, or having to progress methodically through unnecessary steps or parts of the system in order to take a particular action, when the intervening stages are not required.

The interface should be able to accommodate users in different circumstances. This may relate to differing levels of experience, where more experienced users may wish to bypass or suppress certain aspects of the interface, in order to increase speed and efficiency of interaction. Certain needs and requirements may arise due to changes in external circumstances, or to circumstances specific to a particular situation. The interface should allow users the flexibility to adapt to such context-specific situations. This is particularly important for applications which have a very generalized and wide-spread use, where different user groups in different environments may have different needs and requirements.

Caution should be exercised, however, when considering the amount of flexibility to be provided. In some situations, too little flexibility can be extremely frustrating, restrictive and detrimental to speed and efficiency of performance. In others, however, too much flexibility can have an extremely negative effect on performance. For complex interfaces, excessive flexibility may make the interface incomprehensible to the users, and may prevent them from forming a clear understanding of what it does, or of how it works. If too many options or facilities are provided, users may become extremely confused about what they are supposed to do, or even what they can do. Great care should to taken, therefore, to achieve an appropriate amount of flexibility for a particular interface and application.

In all cases, however, the users should feel that they are in control of the system, and that they have choices about the nature of the interaction, wherever possible.

4.7.2   Explanation of flexibility and control checklist questions

Question 1. Is there an easy way for the user to 'undo' an action, and step back to a previous stage or screen? (e.g. if the user makes a wrong choice, or does something unintended)
Some form of 'undo', which allows the user to step back to a previous stage, is extremely important, as there may often be occasions where users wish to change their minds, or find that they have done something unintentional. For less experienced users, the provision of an 'undo' facility will greatly assist their potential for learning about the system; they may have much more confidence about trying a particular action if they are aware that it can be undone.

Question 2. Where the user can 'undo', is it also possible to 'redo' (i.e. to reverse this action)?
It is important that users are offered the opportunity not only to 'undo' actions, but also to reverse this action. For example, a user may have been uncertain about the action or operation carried out, and then changed his or her mind.

Question 3. Are shortcuts available when required? (e.g. to bypass a sequence of activities or screens)
For example, when carrying out a task, the user may wish to move quickly to another part of the system and back again without having to go through the intervening steps. Shortcuts can increase the speed with which more experienced users can use the system.

Question 4. Do users have control over the order in which they request information, or carry out a series of activities?
Where it is not essential for a series of activities to be carried out in a preset sequence, it may be preferable to allow users to choose the

order in which they carry out the activities, as different users may have different preferences.

Question 5. Can the user look through a sequence of screens in either direction?

This is particularly important where the user is looking at a long list or table which covers several screens (or 'pages'). It is extremely frustrating to have to go all the way back to the first page and start scanning again from the beginning if the user wishes to look at the previous page (e.g. go back to page 6 when on page 7).

Question 6. Can the user access a particular screen in a sequence of screens directly? (e.g. where a list or table covers several screens)

As in question 5 above, it is frustrating and time-consuming if the user wishes to look at page 6 out of 12, and has no facility to address that page directly but has to scan through from page 1. This is obviously more important when there are a large number of screens of information.

Question 7. In menu-based systems, is it easy to return to the main menu from any part of the system?

Since the main menu is likely to be the primary point of access to all parts of the system, flexibility can be greatly enhanced if this can be accessed immediately from anywhere in the system. A menu hierarchy can be extremely cumbersome if the user must move up through all levels in the hierarchy, in order to reach the main menu.

Question 8. Can the user move to different parts of the system as required?

Requirements for flexibility of movement between different parts of the system may in some cases only be revealed when carrying out a task.

Question 9. Is the user able to finish entering information (e.g. when typing in a list or table of information) before the system responds? (e.g. by updating the screen)

For example, the user may be entering a long list or table of information which covers several screens and which will need to be sequenced by the computer (e.g. alphabetically, chronologically). If the computer starts resequencing the information after the user has only entered one screen of information, then the user could get confused as to where they are in the list. It would be preferable, in this case, for the computer to wait until the user has entered all information before resequencing.

Question 10. Does the system prefill repeated information on the screen, where possible? (e.g. to save the user having to enter the same information several times)
It can be extremely tedious for the user to have to enter the same information repeatedly through a task (e.g. a name or reference number). The system should be designed such that the same information may be displayed on a number of screens automatically by the computer, once the user has entered it initially.

Question 11. Can the user choose whether to enter information manually, or to let the computer generate information automatically? (e.g. where there are defaults)
For example, there may be situations where numerical data is displayed, such as measurements, for which there are fairly standard default values. Users may wish to use these values, in which case they may prefer to let the computer display them prefilled on the screen. There may also be occasions, however, when users wish to enter totally new information, in which case they may prefer a blank screen. They should have the flexibility to choose.

Question 12. Can the user override computer-generated (e.g. default) information, if appropriate?
Where the computer generates data (e.g. from the database or from calculations) which the user has authority to change, then the user should be able to override this computer-generated data (e.g. due to a change in situation).

Question 13. Can the user choose the rate at which information is presented?
Where users are to be instructed (e.g. in help and tutorial parts of the interface), or are required to consult several screens of information, it is extremely important that they can control the speed at which they receive this information. Users can control the presentation of this type of information (as opposed to being shown the information automatically), for example, with a simple input action to forward the information (e.g. pressing the space bar). However, users may feel that the breaks in the information are unnatural, or that the input response needed is too tedious. It is important that this type of control is chosen with care.

Question 14. Can the user choose how to name and organize
information which may need to be recalled at a later stage? (e.g.
files, directories)
Users' memory load may be reduced when recalling information if
they have named or categorized that information themselves (as
opposed to default naming of files, prescribed directories, etc.).

Question 15. Can users tailor certain aspects of the interface for
their own preferences or needs? (e.g. colours, parameters)
It is important that the user is offered control over some of the basic
features of the interface, where possible.

4.8 CHECKLIST SECTION 8: ERROR PREVENTION AND CORRECTION

The system should be designed to minimize the possibility of user
error, with inbuilt facilities for detecting and handling those which do
occur; users should be able to check their inputs and to correct errors
or potential error situations before the input is processed.

4.8.1 Description of error prevention and correction
This criterion aims to reduce the likelihood of errors as far as
possible, and to ensure that those which do occur are rectified before
they cause problems. Since all users, regardless of their level of
experience, will make errors at some time, the interface should be
designed to prevent errors where possible. This can be achieved for
certain types of error, such as those resulting from unauthorized
actions (e.g. by using passwords), and certain trivial errors (e.g.
entering alphanumeric characters into a numeric field).

However, it is unlikely that all errors can be prevented. The
interface should therefore validate every user input. Where it is able
to detect errors, it should ensure that the user corrects any which are
made before progressing further. It is essential to inform users of
where and what the errors are, and of how to correct them (when the
interface is able to provide such information).

There will also be errors which the interface is unable to detect.
For example, there may be situations where the user takes an action
or enters information unintentionally. Such errors may have serious
consequences for the user if processed. Users should therefore be
given the opportunity to check and correct (or 'undo') all inputs
before processing.

4.8.2   Explanation of error prevention and correction checklist questions

Question 1. Does the system validate user inputs before processing wherever possible?
Where user inputs can be validated by the computer (e.g. where there are set boundaries or limits on what the user can enter, or a set number of options), then the computer should validate the inputs before proceeding further. If this does not happen, then problems may occur later which could have been avoided.

Question 2. Does the system clearly and promptly inform the user when it detects an error?
This relates to informative feedback (Section 4, questions 13 and 14), as 'clearly' depends to a large extent on the quality of error messages.

Question 3. Does the system inform the user when the amount of information entered exceeds the available space? (e.g. trying to key five digits into a four-digit field)
If, for example, a user wants to key '1234' into a four-digit field, but accidentally keys in '01234', then unless the system informs the user of the mistake, the number in the field will continue to read '0123', and this would be likely to cause problems.

Question 4. Are users able to check what they have entered before it is processed?
This is particularly important with regard to inputs which the computer is not able to validate.

Question 5. Is there some form of cancel (or 'undo') key for the user to reverse an error situation?
For example, users may realize they have made an error, perhaps when overtyping or amending a number of information fields on the screen, and may wish to cancel what they have done and start again. This is particularly important where errors are beyond the capability of the system to detect. Such a facility should enable users to step back as far as they require (i.e. if the user wishes to go back several stages, then the system should allow them to do so).

Question 6. Is it easy for the user to correct errors?
This can reflect quality and adequacy of informative feedback (Section 4) and of user guidance and support (Section 9).

Question 7. Does the system ensure that the user corrects all detected errors before the input is processed?
The system should revalidate until the input is corrected, rather than allow the user to proceed.

Question 8. Can the user try out possible actions (e.g. using a simulation facility) without the system processing the input and causing problems?
Some form of simulation (or 'what if. . .') facility can enable users to try out alternative actions safely.

Question 9. Is the system protected against common trivial errors?
Common errors may be typing mistakes, or wrong keys accidentally hit. It can be frustrating for the user to have to spend large amounts of time correcting such errors, or having to be extremely careful in order to avoid them. If the system is designed such that these errors cannot be made (e.g. prevent entry of numerics into an aliphatic field; prevent entry of options other than those available), then this can relieve user frustration and save time.

Question 10. Does the system ensure that the user double-checks any requested actions which may be catastrophic if requested unintentionally? (e.g. large-scale deletion)
Such actions may be intended, but if not then they could cause severe disruption. These actions may be specific to the task or may be actions such as deletion or updating of information. The user should be asked to actively confirm such actions.

Question 11. Is the system protected against possible knock-on effects of changes in one part of the system?
The system should ensure that changes which the user makes do not have unfortunate repercussions elsewhere. If a change may have knock-on effects if processed, then the system should inform the user before continuing any further.

Question 12. Does the system prevent users from taking actions which they are not authorized to take? (e.g. by requiring passwords)
In some situations, a degree of security will be required, and it is important that users are made aware of their restrictions in this respect.

Question 13. In general, are system errors and malfunctions rare?
Errors may not always be caused by the user, and it is important to
identify any errors or malfunctions which may result from problems
with the system. The user should be informed as to the class of error
in such situations.

*Question 14. When system errors occur, can the user access all
necessary diagnostic information to resolve the problem? (e.g.
where and what the fault is, what is required to resolve it)*
There may be cases where a fault must be resolved by a technician.
However, the system should still provide the user with sufficient
information to determine this.

4.9   CHECKLIST SECTION 9: USER GUIDANCE AND SUPPORT

Informative, easy-to-use and relevant guidance and support should
be provided, both on the computer (via an on-line help facility) and in
hard-copy document form, to help the user understand and use the
system.

4.9.1   Description of user guidance and support
It is widely accepted that some form of on-line 'help' facility should be
available to the user, and that users should be able to request 'help'
from any point in the system. The system, in response, should then
explain the options available to the users in the context of what they
are currently doing.

'Help' facilities can provide assistance both to novice users and to
more experienced users — all users tend to forget aspects of a system
after a certain time (Maguire, 1982). The facility should be structured
so that the user can find relevant information directly, without having
to look through unnecessary material. It should also be flexible
enough to allow users to browse through information other than that
specifically required.

On-line guidance also provides a very effective learning tool, if
structured well. Kennedy (1974) comments: 'It is often difficult,
initially, to persuade someone to use a terminal when they are
unsupervised since they have no means of asking questions. If the
user can ask the computer what to do at any stage or to explain how a
particular function works, the process of familiarisation proceeds
fairly rapidly' (p. 319).

Since it is impractical, in most situations, to hold all information
about an interface and its application on the computer, a more in-

depth, comprehensive, up-to-date and well-organized description should be provided in hard-copy form. Written manuals and user guides are often excessively long and complex, and out-of-date. Wright (1981, 1985) has provided a comprehensive review of the problems to be overcome when writing hard-copy documentation, together with some guidance for those creating such documents. User guidance, both on-line and in hard-copy form, provides the flexibility for the interface to support different users, and enables exploration of the different facilities available.

4.9.2 Explanation of user guidance and support checklist questions

Question 1. If there is some form of help facility (or guidance) on the computer to help the user when using the system then:
If an evaluator writes 'not applicable' or fails to answer question 1 when there is some form of on-line guidance, then this implies that the system has not made it sufficiently clear that such a facility exists.

Question 1(a). Can the user request this easily from any point in the system?
The user should be able to call upon the help facility at any stage in an interaction, and from any screen.

Question 1(b). Is it clear how to get in and out of the help facility?
If it is not clear, then this can reflect poor labelling of 'help'; poor visual clarity; poor compatibility with what the user would expect to see for a help facility label; poor consistency within the system or with other systems in terms of where, or in what form, the help indicator appears on the screen; and inadequate informative feedback.

Question 1(c). Is the help information presented clearly, without interfering with the user's current activity?
When carrying out a task, it may become evident that presentation of help information actually disrupts the task. For example, a dialogue box which appears mid-screen and describes different possible actions by reference to the current work items may have obscured those items to which the user must refer.

Question 1(d). When the user requests help, does the system clearly explain the possible actions which can be taken, in the context of what the user is currently doing?
This question is closely related to the task which the user is carrying out. It is extremely important for a help facility to explain the options available to users at their current point in the task.

Question 1(e). When using the help facility, can the user find relevant information directly, without having to look through unnecessary information?
It is important that users are able to access relevant information directly, as this saves time and frustration.

Question 1(f). Does the help facility allow the user to browse through information about other parts of the system?
Where possible, users should not be restricted solely to looking at information relating to what they are currently doing. The ability to browse through information about other sections can be an extremely effective form of learning.

Question 2. If there is some form of hard-copy guide to the system (e.g. user guide or manual) then:

Question 2(a). Does this provide an in-depth, comprehensive description, covering all aspects of the system?
Since it may not always be possible to hold all information about the system on the computer, it is essential that any form of hard-copy documentation should be comprehensive.

Question 2(b). Is it easy to find the required section in the hard-copy documentation?
Hard-copy documentation should be well-organized and well-indexed, so that if users wish to refer to it for a specific piece of information, while carrying out a task, they are able to retrieve the required information easily and quickly.

Question 3. Is the organization of all forms of user guidance and support related to the tasks which the user can carry out?
Users are most likely to refer to user guidance and support facilities within the context of tasks. If the facilities do not relate to the tasks in the way they are organized, then users may have difficulty finding the information they want.

Question 4. Do user guidance and support facilities adequately explain both user and system errors, and how these should be corrected?
Users need to be provided with information on different types of error (both system errors and user errors), on how they are caused and how they can be corrected.

Question 5. Are all forms of user guidance and support maintained up-to-date?

Documentation and other forms of guidance often become out-of-date very quickly, as systems and their interfaces are updated. Users must be provided with the current documentation, and any on-line guidance must incorporate the latest changes.

PART III
How to evaluate a user interface using the method

Part III describes how to use the method in an evaluation.

5. How to construct tasks for the evaluation
This stresses the importance of evaluation tasks as a central part of the method. It describes how to carry out a task analysis, and how to use the information arising from this to construct realistic and representative tasks for use in the evaluation.

6. How to conduct the evaluation
This outlines the various factors to be considered when conducting the evaluation. These include a number of preliminary considerations and some points to note when briefing the evaluators, both before and during the evaluation.

7. How to analyse the results of the evaluation
This describes the information which can be obtained from the evaluation, and how this information can be analysed.

5

How to construct tasks for the evaluation

5.1 WHY USE TASKS IN AN EVALUATION?

Chapter 2 summarized the main reasons for employing tasks in an evaluation. These are restated below, in order to provide the context for the remainder of this chapter.

(1) Tasks which are realistic and representative of the work for which the system has been designed, provide the most effective way of demonstrating the system's functionality.

(2) This enables those evaluating the interface to see it not simply as a series of screens and actions, but as part of the application system as a whole.

(3) By carrying out tasks, evaluators can be exposed to as many aspects of the user interface as possible. This is necessary if they are to comment usefully, and in detail, on specific features, problems, strengths and deficiencies.

(4) Many significant problems and difficulties are only revealed when carrying out tasks.

(5) In some cases, there may be important aspects of usability which can only be captured by using the system.

(6) Important information can be gathered by observing and recording an evaluator's performance when carrying out tasks. This can be extremely valuable in identifying difficulties which evaluators experience when interacting with the system.

The first step in carrying out a user-interface evaluation using the method, therefore, is to construct the tasks to be used in the evaluation.

5.2 OVERVIEW OF EVALUATION TASK CONSTRUCTION

There are two main stages involved in constructing the tasks to be carried out in the evaluation.

(1) Carry out a basic task analysis

This involves:

— gathering information about existing work on similar systems, and about the intended use of the system under evaluation;
— collating and representing this information, so that it can be assessed as a realistic description;
— analysing the description produced, and improving it where necessary.

(2) Develop the evaluation tasks

This involves:

— deciding on the number of tasks to be used;
— appraising the chosen evaluation tasks, in order to check their representativeness, how well they can be performed, and the extent to which they explore the functionality of the system under evaluation;
— carrying out a pilot investigation, improving the evaluation tasks in the light of this.

Each step is described in detail below. The procedure outlined is necessarily general, and this part of the method will be greatly influenced by the context of the evaluation, including, for example, the type of work to be carried out by the system, the system's current state of development, the novelty and complexity of the system, and so on.

5.3 TASK ANALYSIS

The background research which is necessary in order to construct and use evaluation tasks is commonly known as 'task analysis'. Although there are a great many definitions of task analysis, a fairly typical definition is: '...a formal methodology, derived from systems analysis, which describes and analyses the performance demands made on the human elements of a system.' (Drury *et al.*, 1987, p. 371).

Clegg *et al.* (1988) describe the general aim of task analysis as being: 'to split any work activity into its basic elements, each being directed to a particular goal.' (p. 168).

The task analysis need not be especially sophisticated (cf. hierarchical task analysis of process control situations, e.g. Shepherd and Duncan, 1980). It is more important that the essential task elements are identified, so that they can later be combined in a meaningful and realistic way in the form of one or more evaluation tasks.

5.3.1   Information collection

The tasks used in the evaluation must be based on a sound understanding of the work to be carried out using the system. The first stage of a task analysis, therefore, is to gather relevant information in order to construct accurate evaluation tasks. In the simplest case, this will involve understanding what is done, in what order, dependent upon what, and why.

There are a number of critical information sources to which reference should be made. The major sources are listed below, together with the way in which the information might be assessed.

General documentation

Reference should be made to any project documentation outlining the requirements of the system and interface, and the user's role. Where a system is evaluated during development, this might include the orginal information that has been used to create the requirements or functional specifications. In other cases this documentation may take the form of details accompanying 'off-the-shelf' systems. In addition, particular companies may have established procedures or codes for carrying out work, and these should also be consulted.

Operating manuals and training materials

Examine any operating manuals and training materials for the system in question, and from existing systems that are similar in nature and purpose. Consultation of users' training course material is useful in gaining an overview of 'how it is meant to be done' (although this is often very different to how it is done in practice).

Where the system is either at an early stage of development (and instructional material is in a state of infancy), or the system is completely novel (where there are very few similar systems around), this method of information gathering is limited.

Consult end-users

Consult existing and potential end-users about their current work, and about the way they envisage the new system supporting their work. It is preferable to do this either in combination with, or with reference to, observation of users carrying out their normal work (see below).

When consulting users about their work, be sure to fully explain the purpose of the exercise, and to go prepared with a basic comprehension of their work. When asking users about the types of work carried out, structured interviews are usually most useful. Therefore, a structure of questions and themes should be devised prior to consultation.

However, it is not always possible to gain a full picture from users, as they may find it difficult to verbalize their knowledge of the tasks they carry out in the context of their work. This may well be the case in highly skilled work, where users are experts and are so familiar with their work that they find it difficult to explain its fundamental characteristics simply and clearly.

Observation of users at work

Together with the consultation of users, the observation of users carrying out tasks within their normal working environment should form the basis of the task analysis.

Again, the users being observed should be aware of the nature of the investigation, as their cooperation is fundamental to the success of the exercise. The observation should aim to be unobtrusive, in order that the work under investigation is as 'natural' as possible.

During the observation of end-users it is often possible to ask them to 'talk through what they are doing'. In this way it is possible to follow a great deal of what is going on, and more importantly to gain some insight into why certain things are being done (e.g. 'this must be carried out in this sequence because. . .'; 'if I find that this might happen then I should go to. . .'; 'I always need to check this when I have done that').

Related to the observation of users, it is sometimes possible to ask users to construct a simple diary in which to note down their actions when using the system, as well as 'offline' activities. Naturally, the diary needs to have a pre-specified format in which the characteristics of tasks can be documented. User diaries are often a useful means of generating information and questions about tasks, although for some tasks (e.g. involving continuous control) only general retro-spective reports can be obtained.

When observing the tasks people are carrying out, a broad cross-section of users should be involved. Some users may have developed their own way of doing something that is not at all common to the general user group. Also, people at different levels (e.g. users, supervisors, support staff, etc.) will have different perceptions of the nature and goals of some of the tasks. It is important to consult these people and to take into account the range of views.

In many development environments, consultation with end-users, and observation of their work may have already been carried out at the systems analysis stage of the project. Obviously, where the tasks which the system is to carry out are entirely novel, these two techniques for collecting task-related information will be limited.

5.3.2   Representing the task information
When collating and representing the information which has been gathered during task analysis, a number of points should be considered.

(1) Is this representation sufficiently detailed to be able to create generic evaluation tasks?
(2) Is the means of description which has been employed, clear and unambiguous?
(3) Where appropriate, will it be possible to take this representation back to the users, in order for them to usefully comment and further explain, as necessary?

At the end of the task analysis, it should be possible to describe the tasks, sub-tasks, sub-sub-tasks, and so on, so that a complete picture is drawn of what is done, how it is done, and why (and if possible its criticality to the overall task). This must be clearly related to what is done next, to the preceding action, and to any tasks which may be carried out at the same time.

5.3.3   Iteration of the task information
At this stage, it is important, where appropriate, to return to the users who have provided the information, in order to correct and/or embellish the analysis. These users will be able to comment on the proposed description of what they do, and the description can be iterated in order to incorporate further information and explanation.

The level of detail represented should be examined, as it need only be sufficient to enable design of the evaluation tasks. There is always a danger of taking the analysis as far as it will go (in which case a great deal of superfluous information may be generated), rather than to the level required by the evaluation.

5.4   DEVELOPMENT OF THE EVALUATION TASKS(S)

Having produced a satisfactory description of the information gathered during task analysis, the evaluation tasks themselves can now be developed.

5.4.1   Deciding on the number of evaluation tasks

The first step is to establish whether it is important to create one general task that includes many relevant elements, or whether to employ several tasks that 'test' different aspects of the interface and the system. Several factors should be considered. The first consideration is whether it is possible to combine all the relevant elements of work within the system into one large task (this will be affected by the scale and complexity of the system under evaluation). The second consideration is whether or not such a combination would be realistic in terms of the work to be carried out using the system. In some cases there may be tasks which are completely independent of one another, yet are conducted using the same system with the same interface. Finally, it is important to consider whether it will be reasonable to ask evaluators to carry out a large, combined task.

5.4.2   General guidance for developing evaluation tasks

Clearly, there can be no hard and fast way of developing an evaluation task when so many variables exist (from the nature of the application itself, to the time allocated for the evaluation exercise). Some general guidance on what should be considered when translating the task analysis information into the form of a written evaluation task, is provided below. The points which are made are neither exhaustive, nor mutually exclusive. For simplicity in explanation, the assumption has been made that only one task is to be used in the evaluation. However, the same points apply where a number of tasks have been selected.

(1)   The evaluation task should be representative

The task must contain all elements which are important when it is normally carried out. These should be accurately represented, both in terms of their criticality to successful performance of the task, and in terms of their relative occurrence within the task. The overall task must appear as realistic as possible, employing realistic data and, where appropriate, describing a realistic 'problem to-be-solved' using the system. (This is also known as 'face validity').

(2)   The evaluation task should enable successful performance
The task created must be reasonable, so that it can be successfully completed by the majority of those taking part in the evaluation. Should a task appear especially daunting to an evaluator, then his or her cooperation throughout the evaluation, including completion of the checklist, may be made more difficult.

(3)   The evaluation task should cover as much functionality as possible
The task must be reasonably broad in that the required functionality of both the system and the interface must be explored to as great an extent as possible. It is important to note that the evaluation task should test the required functionality, rather than the actual functionality, of the system being evaluated. However, in a development situation, the interface and system may be at a stage of development where only some aspects are sufficiently operational to support an evaluation task.

5.4.3   Pilot and iterate
When checking the adequacy of the tasks developed for the evaluation, a number of trade-offs may be necessary. One of the most useful ways in which to assess these is within a short pilot study. This enables an assessment of whether the tasks to be used in the evaluation meet the general points outlined above. This pilot will involve carrying out the evaluation tasks using the system, preferably with the help of a potential end-user, in order to check whether alterations are necessary.

This is a crucial stage in the development of evaluation tasks. Once the evaluation has begun, it is then too late, for example, to alter a task so that it will make use of a part of the system not currently entered, or to 'trim' a task so that it can be carried out more quickly. The pilot stage offers the last opportunity to modify the evaluation task(s).

5.4.4   Developing instructions for carrying out the evaluation tasks
The final stage within the development of the evaluation tasks is construction of the instructional material explaining the tasks, which is to be presented to evaluators. The instructions must be clear and unambiguous, in order to leave the evaluators in no doubt as to what they must do. The degree of specificity of the instructions will depend on the tasks and the system. For instance, the evaluation may require users to make choices as to how they can go about a task; in other

cases, the evaluation task may require each action to be specified in the instructions.

5.5 SUMMARY OF POINTS TO NOTE WHEN CONSTRUCTING EVALUATION TASKS

(1) Do not underestimate the importance of tasks in the evaluation. They are critical to the overall evaluation, and to obtaining useful feedback through the checklist.

(2) When carrying out a task analysis, be sure to analyse any work currently carried out, as well as that proposed for the system under evaluation.

(3) Ensure that the representativeness of the tasks, the difficulty and time factors involved, and the required functionality of the system under evaluation are assessed.

(4) Always consult a range of end-users, where possible, when preparing the evaluation tasks.

(5) Be prepared to reiterate the task analysis and development as necessary, checking that the evaluation tasks are sufficient for the range of evaluators and the application and system in question.

(6) Construct the instructional materials for carrying out the tasks (e.g. text, diagrams, etc.) carefully, making sure that they are clear and unambiguous.

6

How to conduct the evaluation

6.1 PRELIMINARY CONSIDERATIONS

6.1.1 How to design the evaluation

It is not possible to prescribe exactly how the user interface evaluation should be designed; the most appropriate design will depend largely on situational factors, including the system, the application, the types of evaluator available, and so on. However, the basic considerations when designing the evaluation are likely to concern which evaluators will carry out which tasks, using which interfaces (if the evaluation is comparing a number of alternative interfaces).

One important aim should be to control unwanted variables which may affect the results, and to ensure that the various procedures involved in the evaluation (e.g. instructions to the evaluator, instructions for carrying out the evaluation tasks, recording of task performance, etc.) are standardized.

If there is only one evaluation task to be carried out, and only one interface to be evaluated, then the design is relatively simple, as all evaluators will carry out the same task using the same interface. Where there is more than one task or more than one interface, however, there are a number of points which should be considered.

More than one evaluation task

If all evaluators are to carry out all tasks, then the main consideration is to control for task order. For example, if there are two tasks, then half the participants carry out task A before task B, and the other half carry out B before A. If the evaluators can be separated into different groups, according to expertise, background, or experience, for example, then task order should be balanced within each group.

If this is not the case, then it is important to distribute the tasks evenly between the evaluators. For example, half could carry out task A, and the other half could carry out task B. If there are different groups of evaluators, then it is extremely important to ensure that tasks are balanced between the groups, so that each group carries out each task an equal number of times. For example, with two tasks, half the people in each group should carry out task A, and the other half should carry out task B.

More than one user interface
In the case of a comparative evaluation, several general points can be made. The same tasks should be carried out using each interface, by the same number of people, and the points made above, concerning which evaluators should carry out which tasks, can be applied to each interface separately.

A more important consideration here is which users should evaluate which interface(s). The main option is whether each evaluator uses each interface, or whether each evaluator uses only one interface.

In the first case, the order of exposure to each interface should be balanced between evaluators, or evaluator groups. The advantage of this design is that evaluators will be able to make comparative comments between the alternatives, and to express preferences. The disadvantages are that their opinions of each interface may be biased by the order in which they encounter them, they need to commit a great deal of time, and they may be subject to practice and fatigue effects.

The alternative approach, where each evaluator is exposed to only one interface, has the advantage that evaluators can consider the interface in detail. The disadvantage is that the number of evaluators required is multiplied by the number of interfaces, and that evaluators cannot make relative judgments between the interfaces. It is important to ensure that different evaluator groups are equally balanced between the different interfaces.

6.1.2   Know the 'users': background information on evaluators
The different backgrounds, expertise and experience of evaluators, can provide valuable insights when analysing the results of the evaluation. It is important, therefore, that this information is recorded as part of the evaluation, and gathered before evaluation begins. One means of achieving this, is to draw up some form of brief

'evaluator questionnaire', to be given to the evaluators before they carry out the tasks. This may include, for example, points such as:

Job title
Job description
Experience
— in the task domain (e.g. draughting, project management)
— with computer-based systems
— with alternative user interfaces

Many of the questions asked will depend on the nature of the evaluation, of the evaluators, and of the application. For example, in some situations, it may be important to ask about the evaluator's experience with 'similar' applications, and more specific, context-related questions may therefore be necessary.

Evaluators' background information need not necessarily be obtained in the form of a written questionnaire. A more flexible alternative is a brief interview before beginning the evaluation.

6.1.3   How to record task performance

As mentioned at the beginning of Chapter 5, useful information can be gathered from observing evaluators' performance of tasks, and this information can provide a valuable supplement to the checklists when analysing the results. It is important to monitor and record task performance for each evaluator. Some of the main options for monitoring performance are outlined below. Whichever method is adopted, it should be as unobtrusive as possible.

Observational notes

This is one of the most straightforward recording methods to apply in the evaluation. Note-taking can prove difficult if the aim is to gather as much information as possible. However, it is greatly simplified if structured in some way, by deciding in advance which aspects of the interaction to record. Similarly, it may be useful to have a pre-specified format for note-taking, as unstructured notes can be more difficult to interpret.

Some of the most common formats for observational notes involve a 'count and description' of particular aspects of the interaction, such as evaluator confusions, references to on-line help, common mistakes made, requests for help other than from the system, number of menus entered or major choices made, and so on.

Another method of making notes of this sort, is to format the recording sheets into blocks of time (e.g. one-minute blocks). The evaluator's progress can then be checked against time, allowing an analysis later of those sub-tasks which took a particularly long, or short, time to complete.

One of the disadavantages of making observational notes is that the process can be intrusive, and evaluators may find that they need to become familiar with this.

Audio-taping (using verbal protocols)

In some circumstances, evaluators can be asked to 'talk through' or 'think aloud' as they carry out a task. The advantage of this technique is that it yields a 'verbal protocol' of evaluators' comments about their experience of the interface. This can provide the basis for a detailed investigation of problems and difficulties encountered.

Audiotaping techniques may be employed to differing extents, from occasional comments by evaluators about particular difficulties, and the way they think about the solutions, to a complete commentary on the interaction in as much detail as possible. In the latter case, which will rarely be used, the verbal protocol produced largely replaces the observational notes that could have been taken. Whichever degree of verbal report is desired, standard instructions must be used (see Ericsson and Simon, 1985, for a full account of this type of technique).

It is important to be aware of the limitations of this means of recording. In some cases the evaluation task(s) may involve a large amount of concentration, and evaluators may find it difficult to carry out the task and verbalize at the same time. In addition, evaluators may have difficulty in describing what is happening. If audiotaping is to be used, then careful attention must be paid to its implications, in terms of demands on evaluators, the accuracy of the report, and potential disruption to task performance.

Evaluators' problem diaries

These are structured notes made by evaluators as they proceed with the evaluation task(s). Again, there are advantages and disadvantages with this method.

The main advantages are:

(1) evaluators can be left to carry on with the system whilst the administrator(s) of the evaluation are elsewhere (e.g. attending other evaluators);
(2) evaluators are able to describe in their own words the problems they have experienced;
(3) evaluators may feel less inhibited if they are 'unwatched';
(4) combined evaluator diaries can provide an overall picture of what evaluators consider to be the major difficulties.

However, the disadvantages are:

(1) evaluators may feel reluctant to note down a great number of problems, or may not be motivated to describe them in much detail;

(2) there can be large variations between the diaries produced by different evaluators;

(3) the completion of the evaluation task(s) may well be interrupted by the use of problem diaries;

(4) the use of the diaries requires extra briefing of and instructions to evaluators.

Detailed recording of interactions
There are several options for more detailed recording than problem diaries, verbal reports, or observational notes. The main options include videotaping the interaction (with evaluator input and screen display recorded), and logging the inputs (via control software which simply identifies what is pressed or moved, and when). Whilst such methods will yield much data about the conduct of the task(s), they present a very different picture when analysed than that from, for example, a series of observational notes.

For the majority of user interface evaluations, detailed recording is not typically employed. In part, this is due to the technical and administrative demand on the evaluation, and the complexity of the resulting analysis.

6.2   BRIEFING THE EVALUATORS
The evaluation's success is dependent on the cooperation of the evaluators. Great care should therefore be taken when explaining the details of the evaluation to them. They should be clear as to what is being evaluated and why, why they are involved and what the aim of their involvement is, and what they are expected to do, at all stages of the evaluation. A number of points should be noted when briefing the evaluators, before and during the evaluation.

6.2.1   Briefing before they carry out the task(s)
The relevance of some of the points below will depend on the evaluator, on who is administering the evaluation, on the context of the evaluation, and on the application. However, it is important to be aware of all the points.

(1) Explain why the evaluation is taking place
This involves explaining:

— what the system is;

— who it will be (or is) used by;
— why it is being evaluated, and what the aims of the evaluation are (e.g. evaluating a word-processing package to see if it should be purchased; evaluating a system which needs some modification before implementation, in order to identify areas which require improvement).

(2) Explain why the evaluator has been asked to participate

Evaluators should be able to appreciate why and how their particular background, expertise and experience is of relevance to the system, the application, and the evaluation as a whole. They should also be informed of who the other evaluators are. If there are different groups of evaluators, then the reasons for this should be explained to the user.

(3) Explain how their contribution will benefit the evaluation

This again depends on the context of the evaluation. It should be made clear to the evaluator that feedback from themselves, and from other participants, will form the basis of the evaluation, and that it will play an important part in the decisions which are made (e.g. for improvement, purchase, etc.), as a result of the evaluation.

(4) Explain the evaluation procedure

It is important that evaluators are made aware of how the evaluation is to be carried out and what is expected of them. This involves:

— explaining that they will be asked to carry out a task (or tasks) which provides a good way for them to become familiar with, and to experience, the different aspects of the system, and enables them to use the system as realistically as possible;
— explaining that they will then be asked to complete a checklist, which asks a number of questions about the system.

Participants should also be made aware of the time the whole evaluation is likely to take.

(5) Stress the fact that the evaluator is not being 'tested'

It is extremely important to emphasize that the aim is to assess the system, and not the evaluator. The importance of this cannot be overemphasized, as evaluators can become highly stressed, particularly when carrying out evaluation tasks, if they feel that they are under examination themselves.

(6) Explain the evaluation task(s) in detail

This should include a description of what the tasks are. It may be necessary at this stage to provide a more detailed description of the system itself, of what it does, and of what it will be (or is) used for. This will again depend on the context, and on the evaluator.

The evaluator could be given any written instructions concerning the tasks (see Chapter 5), at this stage.

In certain circumstances, it may be necessary to provide a brief demonstration of the various functions which the system carries out. This will depend on the application. If the system is to be used primarily by novice users, with no training, then it is important for the evaluator to carry out the tasks without guidance. If, however, the system is more complex, for specialist use, and the evaluator is a specialist who would receive some training, then a brief introduction may be necessary.

It is important to stress, again, that the evaluator is not being tested, and that if he or she has difficulty carrying out the tasks, then this represents a problem with the system, which should be made known so that it can be resolved. It should be emphasized that the evaluator should have no problems if the system is performing well.

(7) Explain any monitoring which may take place while they are carrying out the task(s)

This will depend on the monitoring technique which is to be used. If the evaluator is to be recorded with an audio-tape, then it is important to assess whether this is acceptable to them, and if so, to describe what is required in detail. In all cases of monitoring, it is essential firstly to ascertain that the procedure is acceptable to the evaluator, and secondly to explain what it is, and why it is being carried out. Again, it is important to stress that the aim is to identify problems with the system, and not with the evaluator.

(8) Explain that they should try and remember any problems or difficulties which they experience when carrying out the task

It should be made clear that it is important to remember as many points about the system as possible when they are completing the evaluation checklist. Evaluators could be given the opportunity to make notes when carrying out the task(s).

(9) Make sure that they understand the purpose and procedure of the evaluation, and that they have the opportunity to ask any questions

If the evaluator is unsure about any aspect of the evaluation, then it is essential that they are able to ask questions. The questions asked may well indicate that some aspect of the evaluation should be explained more clearly, such as the details of the task(s) to be carried out. Make it clear that they can ask questions any time.

6.2.2   Briefing before they complete the checklist

Once the participant has completed the evaluation task(s), several other points should be explained.

(1) Explain the function of the checklist and its structure

The various sections of the checklist should be explained to the evaluator. Although there are written instructions which accompany the checklist, it may be preferable to explain it verbally. The evaluator should be encouraged to write detailed comments wherever possible, as this helps to explain their answers to the questions. Explain that the evaluator should consider the relevant criterion when answering the questions within each section.

(2) Encourage them to report their views of the interface in detail

Explain that the evaluator should be as critical, or as complementary, as they feel necessary. Stress that the aim is to provide as much feedback as possible, since if problem areas can be highlighted now, then they should be rectified before the system is implemented (or purchased, or developed further, etc.). The participant should be positively encouraged to report any difficulties or problems.

(3) Allow them continued access to the system

Evaluators should be able to access the system when answering the questions, so that they can remind themselves of problems, and can expore other aspects if they wish to do so. This could cause a slight problem if the system is in a relatively early stage of development, with some areas still unwritten or 'bugged'. In this case, it may be necessary to ensure that those areas are protected, or that the evaluator's explorations are supervised.

(4) Allow them to ask questions prior to and during the completion of the checklist

In order that the evaluator feels comfortable about answering the questions, and fully understands the nature of the checklist, a member of the evaluation team must be on hand to answer any questions.

7

How to analyse the results of the evaluation

It is not possible here to specify exactly how to analyse the results, or what to do with the results after the evaluation, as this will depend to a very large extent on the context of the evaluation. Instead, this chapter outlines points to note when analysing the different parts of the checklist, and suggests possible strategies which might be adopted for analysing the results and for comparing the differences between evaluators.

7.1 INTRODUCTION

The main source of information arising from an evaluation using the method is likely to be the completed checklist(s). There is no set formula for deciding whether the responses within a particular evaluator's checklist are favourable or unfavourable toward the system being evaluated; any one checklist may reveal any combination of responses, and the nature of the comments and responses to the open questions in the checklist cannot be predicted. However, as a rough guide to which responses are more acceptable and which are less acceptable, four example sets of responses for a completed checklist are briefly outlined below. These show the 'ideal' and the most unacceptable sets of responses, and, less extreme (and more realistically), a relatively favourable and a relatively unfavourable set of responses.

The 'ideal' completed checklist
Sections 1 to 9: every checklist question answered 'always';
every satisfaction scale rated 'very satisfactory';

Section 10:   all answers indicating 'no problems';
Section 11:   no problems, difficulties, or criticisms indicated;
Comments: all comments would be complimentary.

The most unacceptable completed checklist
Sections 1 to 9: every checklist question answered 'never';
                 every satisfaction scale rated 'very unsatisfactory';
Section 10:   all answers indicating 'major problems';
Section 11:   major problems, difficulties and criticisms throughout;
Comments: all comments would voice criticism, indicating problems.

Relatively favourable completed checklist
Sections 1 to 9: all checklist questions answered either 'always', or 'most of the time';
                 all satisfaction scales rated either 'very satisfactory' or 'moderately satisfactory';
Section 10:   no answers indicating 'major problems', and most answers indicating 'no problems';
Section 11:   no major problems, difficulties or criticisms, and few minor problems indicated;
Comments: most comments would be complimentary, with only a few minor criticisms.

Relatively unfavourable completed checklist
Sections 1 to 9: most checklist questions answered either 'some of the time' or 'never';
                 most satisfaction scales rated either 'moderately unsatisfactory' or 'very unsatisfactory';
Section 10:   most answers indicating 'minor problems' or 'major problems';
Section 11:   a number of major problems, difficulties and criticisms indicated;
Comments: most comments would be critical, indicating problems.

The first two examples are both highly improbable, and even if one evaluator produced a completed checklist which was this extreme, it is very unlikely that another evaluator would rate the same interface in quite the same way.

In general, any questions which are answered 'never', any sections which are rated 'very unsatisfactory' and any 'major problems' require immediate attention.

7.2   INFORMATION WHICH A COMPLETED CHECKLIST MAY PROVIDE

In general, a checklist which has been completed during an evaluation is likely to reveal the evaluator's experience of the interface in terms of:

— major problem areas,
— particular areas requiring improvement,
— particularly good aspects of the interface,
— how successful the interface is in meeting each of the criteria.

The checklist can also reveal more fundamental concerns, such as evaluators' misunderstandings, misinterpretations and confusions concerning, for example, what the system is doing, how it works, how it is structured, what the user should be doing, how the interface relates to the task, and possibly what the function of the task is.

In addition, the points arising from the different checklists completed in the evaluation can be summarized and compared. Different opinions of system usability (e.g. with different problems and ratings of satisfaction), which may arise between different evaluators, or groups of evaluators (e.g. representative users, software engineers), can be identified.

When analysing a completed checklist, a close examination of each aspect of the checklist is required. Important information can be obtained from the different sections, and a number of points should be noted when analysing each section, as follows.

7.2.1   Points to note in the criterion-based sections (1 to 9)

Sections 1 to 9 provide information about the interface in terms of the criteria described in Chapter 4 of this book. This can reveal how well the user interface meets the criterion described at the beginning of each section. Areas where the interface does not meet the criterion and where improvement is necessary can be identified, as can specific aspects of the interface which are causing problems, and those which are particularly successful. It is important to analyse all aspects of a section together, in order to gain an accurate impression of the responses made.

Responses to the checklist questions

The responses to the questions within each of these sections can reveal a wealth of information. The significance of particular questions, and of the responses which the evaluators give to them, may depend on the context of the evaluation, and on who the evaluators are.

The amount of information extracted will depend on the level of detail of the analysis. If the primary aim is to look for major problem areas, then it is likely that most attention will be paid to those questions which have been given poor answers (i.e. 'some of the time', or 'never'), and to any comments indicating problems. However, a more detailed analysis should look at the response to each question, and should involve a detailed assessment of every comment.

Comments written beside the checklist questions

These comments are extremely important when analysing the completed checklist; one of the main aims of the checklist questions is to prompt evaluators to remember specific aspects of the user interface, and specific problems encountered when carrying out the tasks.

Comments can help to explain a particular response, and to relate the question specifically to the user interface being evaluated. When analysing their own completed checklists, evaluators may have difficulty remembering why they gave a particular answer to a question if they did not write the reasons down at the time. Similarly, it may not always be obvious why another evaluator has given a particular answer if no explanation is provided.

Where a part of the user interface is particularly poor or problematic, it may be mentioned in a number of comments within a section, or in more than one section of the checklist. Comments can indicate the exact parts of the interface which are causing problems. They may also indicate the importance of a particular checklist question in the context of the interface (for example, the question may be answered 'never', but the evaluator may comment that this was not important when using the system). In addition, comments written beside a particular question may suggest improvements.

'. . . any comments (good or bad)' at the end of each section

These comments may provide an overall assessment by the evaluator of how well the user interface meets the criterion. They may stress particular questions within the section which identify areas of the interface requiring attention. Similarly, they may indicate particular parts of the interface which the checklist questions in the section have shown to be unsatisfactory, or alternatively extremely good, and they may provide suggestions for improvement.

In addition, this enables the evaluator to mention any aspects of the interface, any problems encountered, or other considerations relevant to the criterion described at the beginning of the section which have not been covered by the checklist questions. It also allows the evaluator to comment on the importance of the questions and the criterion to the particular interface being evaluated (for example, a number of questions may be answered 'some of the time' or 'never', but the evaluator may comment that this was not significant when using the system).

Satisfaction rating at the end of each section

Some caution should be exercised when interpreting the satisfaction rating, as some evaluators may be inclined to give similar ratings (e.g. non-extreme) regardless of the answers they have given to the specific checklist questions, and of whether they have experienced problems. A scan of the ratings within the different sections, and of the problems identified in Section 10, may reveal any such tendency within an individual checklist.

In general, however, these satisfaction ratings can be very revealing. A rating may indicate the relative importance of particular questions within the section, or of the criterion itself, to the usability of the system. For example, the majority of questions in a particular section may be answered 'most of the time' or 'some of the time', with just a few answered 'never', but the rating at the end of the section may indicate 'very unsatisfactory'. This might imply that the cases where questions are answered 'never', are highly important, pointing to aspects of the interface requiring immediate attention.

On the other hand, the rating in a particular section may be 'moderately satisfactory', but there may appear to be a number of questions answered 'some of the time' or 'never'. As mentioned under '. . . any comments' above, this may suggest that these aspects did not cause any particular problems for usability of the system under evaluation.

In general, a section which has been rated 'very unsatisfactory' is likely to indicate problems, while a section which has been rated 'very satisfactory' may indicate particularly successful aspects of the interface.

Other factors to note

Particular attention should be paid to answers where an evaluator has written 'not applicable' or 'N/A'. There may be situations where an evaluator has not been made fully aware of a specific feature of the interface (e.g. the existence of a help facility, or of shortcuts); they may believe the facility is not present, and consequently may enter 'N/A' for a question where this is not correct.

7.2.2   Points to note in Section 10, on usability problems
This section identifies both major and minor problem areas. It is placed at the end of the checklist because questions within Sections 1 to 9 are likely to have drawn the evaluator's attention to the problems encountered when carrying out the evaluation tasks.

Comments written beside the questions
Any comments written in this section are extremely important as they can provide a quick and specific indication of exactly where the user interface requires attention. Similarly, if an evaluator has written comments where there are no problems, then this can provide feedback on good aspects of the system.

Links with Sections 1 to 9
Many of the problems identified in Section 10 may be caused by factors identified in Sections 1 to 9. The questions therefore relate closely to the earlier sections, and in some cases to specific questions within these sections. Table 7.1 at the end of this chapter indicates where the usability problems identified within Section 10 can be cross-referenced to other parts of the checklist.

The table may help to explain a particular satisfaction rating within a section. For example, if there is only one instance of 'never' in a section, but the section has been rated 'very unsatisfactory', then Table 7.1 may show a direct link between a question in Section 10 for which 'major problems' have been indicated and the question answered 'never' in the earlier section. Any earlier sections and questions cross-referenced from problems identified in Section 10 should therefore be examined closely to see if they represent possible causes of the problems.

7.2.3   Points to note in Section 11 (general questions on usability)
Questions 2, 3 and 5 (and possibly question 7) summarize problem areas, areas of difficulty and confusion, and the major causes of mistakes for the evaluator. Question 4 indicates less problematic areas which nonetheless caused irritation to the evaluator when carrying out the tasks. Questions 6 and 7 may give suggestions for improvement. Question 1 (and possibly question 7) can provide a summary of particular strengths of the system identified by the evaluator.

The comments and points made in this section may overlap with those written elsewhere by an evaluator, and may provide a good overview of these other comments. They can provide an immediate

Table 7.1 — Cross-referencing usability problems to other parts of the checklist

Questions on usability problems in Section 10	Related checklist sections (specific question numbers are indicated, where appropriate)								
	1	2	3	4	5	6	7	8	9
1				*	*				*
2				*					*
3								*	* 2
4			*	*	*	*			*
5			*	*	*	* 7			*
6			*		*	*			* 3
7	*	*	*		*				*
8	*								
9	*	10							
10	*	9							
	10	11							
11						* 5 6	*		
12									* 1
13				* 15	*				
14		*	*			* 11			
15				* 9			* 9		
16				* 9 11			*		
17				* 9 11			*		
18		* 13	*	*	*				
19		*				* 1			
20	* 3	* 7 8		*	*				
21							*		
22				* 13 14			* 1 2	*	
23				* 13 14			*	*	* 4
24				* 13 14			*	*	
25		*							

summary of the most satisfactory and successful aspects of the interface, and of the least satisfactory and problematic aspects for the evaluator.

An evaluator may have written many comments elsewhere, indicating dissatisfaction and a number of problems. In this case, Section 11 may help to clarify which of these were major, which caused most difficulty or confusion, which caused most mistakes to be made when carrying out the evaluation tasks, and which caused irritation rather than significant difficulty. On the other hand an evaluator may have written very few, if any, comments elsewhere, and this section will therefore prompt them to do so.

In addition, this section prompts the evaluator to suggest enhan-

BOOKS etc.
CUSTOMER ORDER

Distributor: _____

Name in full: Mr Symons

Address: _____

Branch: _____

Date: _____

Telephone No. 583 1976-

No. 27338

Order taken by: _____

Qty	Title 0132923688	Author	Publisher	H/P	Est. Price
1	Interfaces a Practical	Bartley Ellis			21—
	Evaluating Usability of	Johnson Howard			
	Interactive Systems	Human Computer Interaction			

CASH ☐ ACCOUNT ☐ Till Receipt No: _____ Deposit: _____

OFFICE USE ONLY

Date ordered: 8/8. Ordered from: BD. Order No: 076146 Date Received: _____

Customer notified on: _____ by letter/telephone (delete as appropriate)

By (insert name of asst.): _____

Remarks: _____

cements to the interface, which can be extremely valuable for follow-up improvements. These suggestions are of particular significance where the evaluator is a representative end-user.

7.3   POSSIBLE STRATEGIES FOR ANALYSING A COMPLETED CHECKLIST

A number of different strategies may be adopted for analysing a completed checklist, all equally valid. The approach adopted may depend to a large extent on the circumstances of the evaluation, including the time available and the main objectives of the evaluation.

7.3.1   A 'top-down' analysis

A more general, or 'top-down', analysis may begin with an overall assessment of the user interface from the checklist, perhaps summarizing strengths and weaknesses. Comments made in Section 11, and problems identified with Section 10, may form the starting point for such an analysis. These may highlight particular aspects of the interface causing problems, and a more detailed investigation may then be carried out to examine other instances where those aspects have been highlighted within the checklist.

An investigation of the other sections within the checklist may take place using Table 7.1 as a framework for the analysis. On the other hand, a full investigation, in detail, of each section within the checklist may follow an initial summary, particularly where a large number of different problems have been indicated in Sections 10 and 11.

7.3.2   A 'bottom-up' analysis

A more detailed, or 'bottom-up', examination may investigate the responses to each question within the checklist. This will enable a more comprehensive picture of the interface to be generated, in terms of its success in meeting the goals for user-centred design specified by the criteria and the checklist questions. Such an analysis is likely to yield a highly detailed specification of aspects of the interface requiring improvement, amendment, addition and enhancement, for example.

A detailed analysis of each of the criterion-based sections will enable a summary to be drawn of the interface in terms of each of the criteria. It may also highlight aspects of the interface which are shown to cause problems repeatedly through these sections. These may also be identified within Sections 10 and 11. A bottom-up analysis can therefore provide not only a comprehensive, detailed assessment, but can also enable this information to be summarized in a number of different ways.

7.3.3 How the context of the evaluation may influence the strategy

The strategy for analysis may be dictated by the aims and the context of the evaluation, and by the amount of alteration which can be carried out on the interface.

For example, an evaluation taking place early in the design process may require a detailed investigation of every question within the checklist, in order to ensure that the next stage of design improves the interface in as many ways as possible and incorporates as many of the points arising from the evaluation as it can.

Alternatively, there may be certain known problem areas within a fully developed system which must be eliminated before the system is implemented. The aim of the evaluation may therefore be to identify exactly what and where these problems are in more detail. An analysis of the results in this situation is likely to concentrate primarily on the aspects of the checklist concerned specifically with these problem areas. Case Study 2 in the Appendix describes a similar situation to this. Prior to the evaluation, it was known that there were a number of problems with the system, although it was unclear as to whether these were related. An initial, general analysis of the completed checklists after the evaluation revealed that the major problems were error-related. This led to a detailed investigation of Section 8 (error prevention and correction), and of related questions elsewhere in the checklist (using Table 7.1).

Where a system is being evaluated with a view to purchase, the primary objective of the evaluation may be to identify the main strengths and weaknesses, and the main areas causing problems. A more general, high-level analysis of the results may be sufficient in this case. For example, if there are a large number of problems, and few strengths, it is unlikely that the system will be purchased, and a detailed analysis of each question within the checklist will not be necessary. Similarly, if a choice is to be made between alternative systems (or interfaces), then it may be possible to make a decision between them based on the relative strengths and weaknesses of each.

7.4 ANALYSING DIFFERENCES BETWEEN EVALUATORS

One of the main aims of the method described in this book is to enable a variety of people, preferably from representative user groups, to evaluate the same user interface in a systematic manner. There should therefore be a number of completed checklists to analyse at the end of an evaluation.

It is important to analyse each checklist individually, and to compare the completed checklists, in order to gain a full assessment of the user interface from all evaluator perspectives. Comparison of the completed checklists can identify where evaluators differed in their perceptions and experience of the interface, and in the problems which they encountered. Different evaluators may identify different, but equally important, problems with the interface. It is important to stress that no single assessment of the interface is 'right' or 'wrong'. Evaluators may produce very different results but these are all equally valid.

There are two issues of importance here. The first concerns what differences there are between the evaluators' checklist results; and the second concerns what reasons there are, if any, for these differences.

7.4.1   Comparing the different checklists

Again, a top-down or bottom-up strategy may be adopted in order to compare the different checklist results. A top-down approach may highlight factors which are common across the checklists, such as particular problem areas or particular strengths, for example. It may also highlight areas where the checklists differ or disagree. This might lead to a more detailed examination of the individual checklists to see if these differences can be identified in more detail.

A bottom-up analysis will allow a detailed comparison against each of the criteria. For example, one evaluator may rate informative feedback (Section 4) as being 'moderately satisfactory', and give responses to the questions within that section which are relatively favourable. Another evaluator, however, may rate the same criterion as being 'moderately unsatisfactory', and give responses to the questions within that section which indicate a number of problems.

Case Study 1 in the Appendix describes how different evaluators may experience and reveal different problems.

7.4.2   Investigating possible reasons for the differences

Where there are significant differences between evaluators, it is important to investigate why. It is not possible to stipulate here exactly how to do this, as the number of potential differences and reasons is unlimited. However, a number of factors should be considered.

Firstly, the backgrounds of the differing evaluators can be analysed (e.g. from an 'evaluator questionnaire' completed before the evaluation — see Chapter 6). It is possible that the differences depend on whether the evaluator is a representative user or a software engineer, for example. Alternatively, they may depend on previous experience which the evaluator may have with similar computer applications, or within the application domain; more 'naive' evaluators, for example, may have more problems with certain aspects, such as lack of informative feedback, than more 'experienced' evaluators.

A careful investigation of the information obtained from monitoring the evaluators while carrying out the tasks may shed more light on why the differences in checklist results have occurred. This may reveal instances where the evaluators experienced exactly the same problems when carrying out the tasks, but have completed the checklist differently!

Other factors which should be considered include the design of the evaluation. It is possible that evaluators carrying out different tasks during the evaluation have experienced different problems, or that there is an 'order effect', where evaluators carrying out task A before task B, for example, have experienced different problems to those carrying out the tasks in the opposite order. In these cases, the information gathered during monitoring of the evaluators can be extremely important.

7.4.3 What to do with differing results

The aim of the evaluation is to obtain as much feedback as possible. If evaluators differ, then this should not be a problem. It may be that the evaluators have, together, succeeded in covering more problems than any one of them would have covered alone. It should be remembered that the most important evaluators are those who will actually use the system (or who represent these eventual end-users).

Exactly what to do in the event of significant differences between evaluators will depend on the nature of these differences and the reasons behind them, and on the context of the evaluation. If, for example, a system is being evaluated with a view to purchase and a number of representative users experienced serious problems with it, then, unless those problems can be overcome with training, it is unlikely that the system will be suitable for purchase. Where the system can be amended (e.g. during development), then it is important to ensure that changes made to overcome problems experienced by some evaluators do not cause problems for others.

7.4.4   Analysing the results with a large number of evaluators
Where interfaces are being designed for use by a large cross-section of end-users, involvement of as many of the representative user group as possible may mean that a detailed analysis of every completed checklist is not feasible.

What is important in these situations, however, is to determine the relative frequency with which different responses occur across the completed checklists. This will enable an assessment of where:

— evaluators are most in agreement;
— evaluators have found problems, both major and minor;
— evaluators have found 'no problems'.

Case Study 3 in the Appendix describes such an evaluation. The method of analysis employed provides an example of how the results can be summarized across the checklists.

Appendix: Case studies

The case studies briefly illustrate the application of the method in three different situations. Each case study highlights different aspects of the method.

Case Study 1 illustrates the value for interface designers of using the method and of receiving feedback from others during interface development, and the different problems which can be revealed through the checklist by evaluators with different backgrounds.

Case Study 2 illustrates how one particular criterion-based section of a completed checklist can be analysed and cross-referenced to other parts of the checklist, and the conclusions which can be drawn from such an analysis.

Case Study 3 illustrates a comparative evaluation of three alternative interfaces. It demonstrates how such an evaluation, using the method, can be designed and administered with a large number of evaluators, and how the evaluation results can be summarized and analysed across a large number of completed checklists.

A.1 CASE STUDY 1: A PROTOTYPE SCHEDULING PACKAGE

The system described in this case study was in an advanced state of development when evaluated. However, the software engineer who had designed and developed it had received no input from human factors specialists or others.

This case study illustrates the importance of the method for interface designers, including the value of receiving feedback from others during development. It also indicates how different problems can be revealed, through the checklist, by evaluators with different backgrounds.

A.1.1   The system

The system being evaluated was a prototype scheduling and control software package, which formed part of a demonstration transportation system. This was developed within a manufacturing environment as part of a major ESPRIT (European Strategic Programme of Research and Development into Information Technology) project. It consisted of a number of pallets carrying components for assembly passing around a conveyor network, and being diverted to various workstations for processing as required. The layout of the transportation system is shown in Fig. 1.

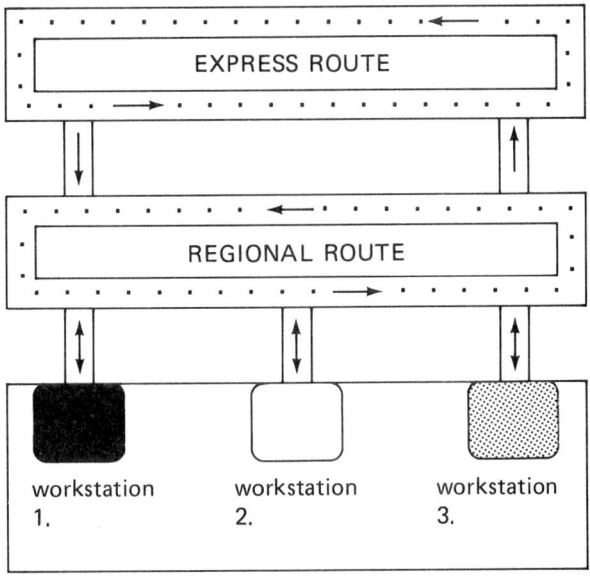

Fig. 1 — Layout of the prototype transportation system, showing direction of pallet movement.

The prototype software, running on an industry-compatible stand-alone microcomputer, allowed loading and editing of schedules, diversion of pallets to the various workstations, monitoring of pallet transportation and diagnosis of problems within the network. Once a schedule had been issued, the system conveyed relevant pallets from the express routeway onto a regional route, and thence to the appropriate workstation. Each pallet was identified using a binary bar code, and code readers were strategically placed within the system. The primary purpose of the demonstration was to illustrate the operation of the conveyor network, and therefore only non-operational 'dummy' workstations were included.

The user interface to the prototype software was relatively uncomplicated in structure (compared with commercial computer-aided production scheduling systems). Navigation through the software was via menus (using letter codes) and cursor keys.

A.1.2 The evaluation

Three different 'groups' of evaluators took part: the software engineer responsible for development of the prototype (both hardware and software); other software engineers, unfamiliar with the prototype; and human-factors specialists, working in the area of human computer interaction. As this was a small-scale demonstration system, no representative end-users (i.e. shop-floor personnel) participated in the evaluation.

Each evaluator carried out two tasks using the system. These were chosen to make use of nearly all options within the software, and involved loading and editing schedules, monitoring movement of pallets around the network and diagnosis of problems within the network.

The evaluator was asked to comment during completion of the task. Having carried out the tasks, the evaluator was then asked to complete the checklist, with the prototype software system available for reference throughout.

Although certain aspects of the interface were shown to be very successful, a number of problems were revealed through the evaluation tasks, the checklist, and the involvement of different people in the evaluation. These problems will not be described in detail here. However, several important factors relevant to the method described in this book were highlighted through the evaluation and are outlined below.

A.1.3 Benefits gained by the interface designer from the evaluation

Some of the more important points to arise from the evaluation were the value of carrying out the evaluation tasks and completing the checklists, and of receiving feedback from others, in exposing unforeseen problems and unsatisfactory aspects to the actual interface designer. Several specific issues arising from the evaluation serve to illustrate this.

Use of colour

In order to make the screens aesthetically pleasing to look at, the interface designer used colour at every opportunity, with a large number of colours on each screen. The other evaluators, unfamiliar with the screens, all found the excessive number of colours extremely confusing. Feedback from the checklists completed by the other evaluators, therefore, revealed that the designer's attempt to enhance the appearance of the screens had actually reduced visual clarity for the user.

Menu position

In an attempt to maintain consistency, the interface designer assigned a set location on the screen for each type of menu. This meant that different menus appeared in different parts of the screen. However, although the designer had no difficulty in knowing where to expect a particular menu when carrying out the evaluation tasks, other evaluators had considerable problems, and found that the menus 'kept changing position on the screen . . . all over the place . . . didn't know where to look'.

Flexibility

The benefits of basing the approach on realistic tasks was clearly illustrated with respect to flexibility. While carrying out the diagnosis task, all evaluators, including the designer, found that they needed to monitor two workstation junctions on the network concurrently; the interface only allowed monitoring of one junction at a time.

An additional issue concerning flexibility arose when a seemingly satisfactory and potentially flexible menu structure proved to be extremely rigid, inflexible and 'cumbersome' — the interface designer's words — when trying to complete the evaluation tasks.

A.1.4. Benefit of involving evaluators from different backgrounds

The benefits of obtaining a range of user perspectives through the evaluation was demonstrated by a review of the completed checklists, which revealed that the evaluators within the different 'groups' (i.e. from different backgrounds) experienced slightly different problems. One particular example demonstrates this.

Data entry

This concerned the visual clarity checklist question 'When the user enters information on the screen, is it clear where the information should be entered?' (Section 1, question 3(a)). None of the software engineers experienced problems with this issue. However, a number of the human factors experts had problems, and answered the question with 'never'. These evaluators were more likely to be representative of the eventual users of such a system in a production setting. This therefore emphasizes the need for input from other sources, preferably representative end-users, in order to identify all aspects of the interface which could potentially cause problems for those who will use it.

A.1.5   Summary
When working through the checklists, the interface designer was surprised to find that he had not achieved many of his well-intentioned aims for ease of use. He felt that the checklists highlighted many potential areas for improvement, and the feedback from the other evaluators gave him a clearer view of the user's perspective.

A.2   CASE STUDY 2: A PROJECT MANAGEMENT SYSTEM

This case study illustrates how one particular criterion-based section of a completed checklist can be analysed and cross-referenced to other parts of the checklist, and the conclusions which can then be drawn from such an analysis.

A.2.1   The system
The system under evaluation was a project management information package, running within a well-known application-development environment. The package had been developed in-house, for use in a number of different departments within the company. However, it was not satisfactory in its current state, and improvements were thought to be necessary before it could be implemented. In order to identify where and what these improvements should be, a group of representative end-users (i.e. project managers from the different departments) evaluated the package, using the checklist-based method described.

The system allowed, for example, loading of project information into the system, identification of critical paths and time-scales, allocation of resources, and so on.

A.2.2   The evaluation
Each evaluator entered a detailed project plan into the system, together with various other parameters, and then carried out a number of tasks, which would normally be undertaken during a practical project-management exercise.

While carrying out the tasks, the evaluators made a note on paper of any particular problems encountered, and any specific comments which they felt should be made about the interface. They then each completed a checklist, referring back to their notes and to the system, and ensuring that they wrote comments to expand and explain their responses to questions wherever possible.

A review of the completed checklists revealed that, although there were minor variations in responses, the evaluators were in general agreement over the main problem areas. It was evident that one of the weakest parts of the system was in the area of error prevention and correction.

The remainder of this case study analyses one particular ('sample') evaluator's checklist in further detail. The analysis focuses specifically on the error prevention and correction section of the checklist to illustrate how the answers to questions, the satisfaction rating, comments, and cross-referencing to other parts of the checklist can clarify what and where the problems were.

A.2.3   Error-related problems in the 'sample' checklist
Section 8: Error prevention and correction checklist questions
Points of interest in this section are described below.

(1) The satisfaction scale was rated 'moderately unsatisfactory'.
(2) Under 'any comments' at the end of the section, the evaluator wrote 'needs a cancel key to correct errors after entry'.
(3) Question 5 ('Is there some form of cancel (or 'undo') key for the user to reverse an error situation?') was answered 'never'; this is reinforced by the comment described in (2).
(4) Question 8 ('Can the user try out possible actions without the system processing the input and causing problems?') was answered 'never'.
(5) Question 10 ('Does the system ensure that the user double-checks any requested actions which may be catastrophic if requested unintentionally?') was answered 'never'; the evaluator also added the comment 'can purge files too easily'.
(6) Question 2 ('Does the system clearly and promptly inform the user when it detects an error?') was answered 'some of the time', with the added comment 'not always clearly and not always promptly'.
(7) Question 3 ('Does the system inform the user when the amount of information entered exceeds the available space?'), was answered 'some of the time'; here the evaluator added the comment 'on data input screen, can run across to next entry field without realising it'.
(8) Question 6 ('Is it easy for the user to correct errors?') was

answered 'some of the time', and the evaluator added the comment 'not during processing'.

Cross-referencing with Table 7.1

Using Table 7.1, Section 8 can be cross-referenced to question 22 ('Having to be very careful in order to avoid errors'), question 23 ('Working out how to correct errors'), and question 24 ('Having to spend too much time correcting errors') in Section 10, on usability problems. The evaluator indicated 'minor problems' in response to all three questions.

Additionally, the evaluator identified 'major problems' with question 16 in Section 10 ('Information which does not stay on the screen long enough for you to read it'), and added the comment 'error messages'.

Table 7.1 can also be used to cross-reference a number of questions in other sections of the checklist, which may relate to these issues. Within the 'sample' checklist, the evaluator made responses to these related questions which were similar to those already described.

(1) In Section 4 (Informative feedback), the evaluator answered 'never' to both question 13 ('Do error messages clearly explain where and what the errors are and why they have occurred?'), and question 14 ('Is it clear to the user what should be done to correct an error?'). In addition, question 1 in this section ('Are instructions and messages displayed by the system concise and positive?') was answered 'some of the time', with the added comment 'error messages too quick and meaningless'. The evaluator reinforced this when asked for 'any comments' at the end of the section, with the comment 'poor error messages'.

(2) In Section 9 (User guidance and support), the evaluator answered 'some of the time' to question 4 ('Do user guidance and support facilities adequately explain both user and system errors, and how these should be corrected?'), with the comment 'error message explanations not always clear'.

Section 11: General questions on usability

In answer to question 2 ('What are the worst aspects of the system for the user?'), two comments made by the sample evaluator are of interest: the first describes a 'lack of error information', and the second describes a 'lack of ability to correct errors after data entry'.

In answer to question 5 ('What were the most common mistakes you made when using the system?'), the evaluator commented 'typing errors detected too late'.

A.2.4   Summary of the sample evaluator's error-related problems
Several main problems can be summarized from the checklist data
outlined above.

(1) The system does not provide sufficient protection from errors,
either for the system or for the user. It is too easy for the user to
take catastrophic actions such as accidentally purging all files, as
the system does not ensure that the user double-checks such
major actions. The system does not always promply inform the
user of simple typing errors (e.g. on the data input screen) when
these are made. The system provides no facility with which the
user can try actions out before processing (e.g. in simulation).

(2) The system provides inadequate information to the user concerning errors. Error messages often do not stay on the screen long
enough to be read. They are often meaningless, and do not
explain where or what the errors are, why they were caused, or
how to correct them. Explanations of error messages within the
on-line user guidance facility (there was no hard-copy system
documentation available for the system) are not always clear.

(3) There is no 'cancel' or 'undo' facility with which users can correct
errors after data entry.

As a result of these problems, users have to be very careful in
order to avoid errors, since these are fairly easy to make. It is difficult
to correct errors during processing, and users have to spend too much
time correcting errors at a later stage, which were not detected by the
system when they were made.

The only major problem concerning these issues was that error
messages often disappeared from the screen before the user was able
to read them. However, there is obviously a need to improve the
system's ability to validate and detect errors, to improve the timing
and quality of error messages, and of error explanations within the
on-line 'help' facility, and to provide some form of 'cancel' or 'undo'
facility with which the user can efficiently correct errors during data
entry before they are processed.

**A.3   CASE STUDY 3: USER INTERFACES TO A PUBLIC
DATABASE**

This describes the evaluation of three prototype user interfaces to a
large public-access database system. The aim of the exercise was to
assess user reactions to the usability of the three prototypes, and to
detail the strengths and weaknesses of each in order that a subsequent

improved interface could be developed. The number of evaluators taking part in the evaluation was large (61).

The case study illustrates how a comparative evaluation using the method can be designed and administered with a large number of evaluators. It also demonstrates how the evaluation results can be collated, analysed and summarized across a large number of completed checklists.

A.3.1 The systems
The database held information on a number of educational topics of interest to the general public. The three user interfaces to the database were developed independently and concurrently, with the stated intention of being 'user-friendly'.

Each prototype relied upon fairly recent user-interface technology, with coloured text and graphic displays, icons, windows and either a touch-screen or a touch pad.

The systems were supported by stand-alone industry-compatible microcomputers without their conventional 'QWERTY' keyboards. The database information was stored on the 'hard' disk.

A.3.2 The evaluation
The end-user group for the system was to be the general public. The evaluator sample comprised 61 unpaid volunteers who were representative of this eventual end-user group.

The evaluators varied with respect to age and experience with computers, with a broad range of backgrounds. For example, the sample included redundant mineworkers, junior shop assistants, computer science students, hairdressers, caretakers, students with learning difficulties, secretaries, teachers and unemployed people.

Task development
The tasks used in the investigation were constructed to simulate realistic and typical tasks which might be undertaken by the users of the proposed database system. Three tasks were devised, ranging from specific database searching, to unconstrained browsing of the database information, as would be likely in everyday use.

Search Task 1 involved the evaluator selecting a specified topic of information, and then refining the search with two further search parameters. This therefore involved the input of a minimum of three search parameters followed by a browse and consultation of details. Search Task 2 again required the evaluator to find a general topic and to refine the search via two further parameters (different to those in Task 1). However, relative to search task 1, this search was specific, with only one possible solution. The browsing task (Task 3) was unconstrained and was carried out for approximately 15 minutes, evaluators selecting items of interest within the system and then following them through the database to gain further details.

The tasks were developed with reference to all relevant documentation and usage of similar systems in the field. The tasks devised were then examined within the context of a pilot study with six end-users, and modified accordingly.

Design and procedure for the evaluation

The design of the evaluation exercise is shown schematically in Fig. 2. Evaluators were randomly allocated to cells within this design, each user attempting either a browsing or searching task, on one of the three prototype user interfaces. No evaluator was exposed to more than one user interface, or completed more than one of the three evaluation tasks using that system.

Task		Interface X	Interface Y	Interface Z
Browsing				
Searching	Search Task 1			
	Search Task 2			

Fig. 2 — Design of the evaluation.

As far as was possible, the user interface conditions (X, Y and Z) were balanced, as were the two task types; namely, browsing (B) and searching (S). Within the searching tasks, the two searches (S1, S2) were also balanced.

The procedure for the study was as follows. Each evaluator was taken to one of the three prototype interfaces and seated before it. All systems remained switched on, showing their respective 'starting screens'. The evaluator was then informed of the nature and purpose of the study. The reason for the study was emphasized; evaluators were assured that the investigation's aim was an evaluation of the prototype systems and not of the participants. The study was conducted in a relatively informal atmosphere. The evaluator was put at ease, told about the procedure, and then asked if there were any questions.

Prior to beginning a task, the evaluator was given a short form to complete, which requested background information such as age, gender, occupation, experience with computing systems, and previous use of an existing system, which performed similar functions. A section was set aside on the form so that evaluators could note down any comments, queries or criticisms of the system which they might have as they were going through the set task. The evaluator was then presented with the task, and given the opportunity to ask any questions of clarification.

Whilst evaluators carried out the task, general observational notes on the interaction were made by a member of the evaluation team. These notes covered:

— references to 'help' facilities,
— incorrect task actions,
— comments made by the evaluator during the task,
— major problems and difficulties experienced.

Following completion of the task, the evaluator was asked to complete the checklist, and was encouraged to make further use of the system if this was necessary in order to answer specific questions posed by the checklist. A member of the evaluation team was available to answer any queries about the prototype, the task, and the checklist questions.

Each session, including briefing, carrying out the task, and completion of the checklist, lasted for approximately 40 minutes.

A.3.3 Collating and analysing the results

Due to the large number of evaluators, the results were summarized for each user interface using percentage responses. This is briefly described below.

An unmarked, 'master' copy of the first 10 sections of the checklist was used to collate the responses across the completed checklists. The responses from each checklist (except for comments), were marked on the master copy.

The percentage of each possible response to each question was then calculated (the denominator for each question was the number of evaluators answering that question; not all questions were answered by all evaluators). For example, for each question in Sections 1 to 9, the percentage of evaluators answering 'always', the percentage answering 'most of the time' and so on, was calculated. These percentages were marked on another 'master' copy. In this way, a master copy showing percentage responses was drawn up for each interface. From these masters, it was then possible to assess, for each user interface, where:

— evaluators were most in agreement;
— evaluators experienced most problems, both major and minor;
— evaluators experienced least problems.

For each user interface, a scan was carried out of all comments made within the completed checklists, and of all responses to questions in Section 11. Any particular difficulties noted by evaluators, any particularly favourable points made, and any frequently occurring points were extracted and summarized.

In addition, difficulties encountered by evaluators were extracted from the notes made when monitoring them during completion of the tasks, as were any other frequently occurring or important points noted.

Tables of strengths and weaknesses were then drawn up for each user interface. These were compared in detail, allowing recommendations to be made concerning which aspects of each interface should be retained, which aspects were poor, and which required improvement. These comparisons then enabled a specification for an improved user interface to be developed.

A.3.4 Summary of the case study

This case study is primarily concerned with the procedural issues involved in using the method to carry out a comparative evaluation with a large number of evaluators. It therefore illustrates how the evaluation was designed and carried out, how the results were collated, and how they were analysed and summarized. It does not attempt to describe what the results were, and what conclusions were drawn.

References

Clegg, C. W., Warr, P. B., Green, T. R. G., Monk, A., Kemp, N., Allison, G., and Lansdale, M. (1988) *People and computers — how to evaluate your company's new technology.* Ellis Horwood, Chichester.

Drury, C. G., Paramore, B., Van Cott, H. P., Grey, S. M., and Corlett, E. N. (1987) Task Analysis. In Salvendy, G. (ed.) *Handbook of human factors.* John Wiley & Sons, Chichester, pp. 370–401.

Ericsson, K. A. and Simon, H. A. (1985) Verbal reports as data. *Psychological Review,* **67** 215–251.

Galitz, W. O. (1980) *Human factors in office automation.* Life Office Management Assoc., Atlanta, GA.

Gardner, M. M. and Christie, B. (eds) (1987) *Applying cognitive psychology to user-interface design.* John Wiley & Sons, Chichester.

Gould, J. D. and Lewis, C. (1985) Designing for usability: key principles and what designers think. *Communications of the ACM,* **288** (3), 300–311.

Kennedy, T. C. S. (1974) The design of interactive procedures for man–machine communication. *International Journal of Man--Machine Studies,* **6** 309–334.

McCormick, E. J. and Sanders, M. S. (1983) *Human factors in engineering and design,* Fifth edition. McGraw-Hill, New York.

Maguire, M. (1982) An evaluation of published recommendations on the design of man–computer dialogues. *International Journal of Man–Machine Studies,* **16** 237–261.

Mumford, E. (1983) *Designing participatively.* Manchester Business School, England.

Oborne, D. (1982) *Ergonomics at work.* John Wiley & Sons, Chichester.

Shepherd, A. and Duncan, K. D. (1980) Analysing a complex task. In Duncan, K. D., Gruneberg, M. M., and Wallis, D. (eds) *Changes in working life.* John Wiley & Sons, Chichester, pp. 137–150.

Shneiderman, B. (1987) *Designing the user interface: strategies for effective human–computer interaction.* Addison-Wesley, Reading, MA.

Smith, S. L. and Mosier, J. N. (1986) *Guidelines for designing user interface software.* The Mitre Corporation, Beford, MA., USA. Report No. MTR-10090, ESD-TR-86-278.

Wright, P. (1981) Problems to be solved when creating usable documents. Paper presented at IBM Software and Information Usability Symposium, September 15–18th, 1981, Poughkeepsie, NY.

Wright, P. (1985) Prerequisites of writing for computer users. Research Memorandum, MRC Applied Psychology Unit, Cambridge, England.

Bibliography

The bibliography presents a selection of contemporary texts which provide further reading on some of the topics covered in the book. For simplicity, they have been divided into four broad sections: general texts on human–computer interaction and human factors; user interface design; evaluation; and task analysis.

(1) GENERAL TEXTS ON HUMAN–COMPUTER INTERACTION AND HUMAN FACTORS

Badre, A. and Shneiderman, B. (eds) (1982) *Directions in human/ computer interaction.* Ablex Publishing, Norwood, NJ.

Baeker, R. M. and Buxton, W. A. S. (eds) (1987) *Readings in human–computer interaction.* Morgan Kaufman, Los Altos, CA.

Card, S. K., Moran, T. P., and Newell, A. (1983) *The psychology of human–computer interaction.* Lawrence Earlbaum Associates, Hillsdale, NJ.

Carroll, J. M. (ed.) (1987) *Interfacing thought — cognitive aspects of human–computer interaction.* MIT Press, Cambridge, MA.

Christie, B. (ed.) (1985) *Human factors of the user-system interface.* North-Holland, Amsterdam.

Coombs, M. J. and Alty, J. L. (eds) (1981) Computing skills and the user interface. Academic Press, London.

Curtis, B. (ed.) (1981) *Human factors in software development.* IEEE, New York.

Damodaran, L., Simpson, A., and Wilson, P. (1980) *Designing systems for people.* NCC Publications, Manchester.

Hartson, H. R. (1985) *Advances in human–computer interaction*, Volume I. Ablex Publishing, Norwood, NJ.

Monk, A. (ed.) (1985) *Fundamentals of human–computer interaction*. Academic Press, London.

Nickerson, R. S. (1986) *Using computers: human factors in information systems*. MIT Press, Cambridge, MA.

Norman, D. A. and Draper, S. W. (1986) *User-centred system design: new directions in human–computer interaction*. Lawrence Earlbaum Associates, Hillsdale, NJ.

Rubinstein, R. and Hersch, H. (1984) *The human factor — designing computer systems for people*. Digital Press, Burlington, MA.

Salvendy, G. (ed.) (1987) *Handbook of human factors*. John Wiley & Sons, Chichester.

Sime, M. E. and Coombs, M. J. (1983) *Designing for human–computer interaction*. Academic Press, London.

Smith, H. T. and Green, T. R. G. (eds) (1980) *Human interaction with computers*. Academic Press, London.

Thomas, J. C. and Schneider, M. L. (eds) (1984) *Human factors in computer systems*. Ablex Publishing, Norwood, NJ.

Vassiliou, Y. (ed.) (1984) *Human factors and interactive computer systems*. Ablex Publishing, Norwood, New Jersey.

(2) USER INTERFACE DESIGN

Ehrich, W. and Williges, R. C. (eds) (1986) *Human–computer dialogue design*. Elsevier, Amsterdam.

Gardner, M. M. and Christie, B. (eds) (1987) *Applying cognitive psychology to user–interface design*. John Wiley & Sons, Chichester.

Rubin, T. (1988) *User interface design*. Ellis Horwood, Chichester.

Shneiderman, B. (1987) *Designing the user interface: strategies for effective human–computer interaction*. Addison-Wesley, Reading, MA.

Smith, S. L. and Mosier, J. N. (1986) *Guidelines for designing user interface software*. The Mitre Corporation, Bedford, MA, USA. Report No. MTR-10090; ESD-TR-86-278.

(3) EVALUATION

Clegg, C. W., Warr, P. B., Green, T. R. G., Monk, A., Kemp, N., Allison, G., and Lansdale, M. (1988) *People and computers — how to evaluate your company's new technology*. Ellis Horwood, Chichester.

Meister, D. (1986) *Human factors testing and evaluation*. Elsevier, Amsterdam.

(4) TASK ANALYSIS

Annet, J., Duncan, K. D., Stammers, R. B., and Gray, M. J. (1971) *Task analysis.* Training Information No. 6, H.M.S.O., London.

Fleishman, E. A. and Quanitance, M. K. (1984) *Taxonomies of human performance — the description of human tasks.* Academic Press, London.

Gael, S. (ed.) (1988) *The job analysis handbook for business, industry and government*, Volumes I and II. John Wiley & Sons, Chichester.

Patrick, J., Spurgeon, P., and Shepherd, A. (1987) *A guide to task analysis — applications of hierarchical methods.* Occupational Services, Aston, Birmingham.

Wilson, M. D., Barnard, P. J., and Maclean, A. (1986) *Task analysis in human–computer interaction.* Human Factors Report, HF 122, August 1986, Unrestricted. Hursley Human Factors Laboratory, IBM UK Laboratories Ltd., Winchester.

Index